# WALKING THE GREAT VIEWS

# WALKING
# THE GREAT VIEWS

## Roland Smith

*Photographs by John Cleare*

*Maps by Mark Richards*

DAVID & CHARLES
Newton Abbot · London

*To Val, Claire, Neil and Iain,*
*my best friends*

*(pp6–7)*
*The view looking south down the length of Windermere,*
*England's largest lake, from the rocky summit of Todd*
*Crag. Orrest Head, another fine viewpoint, breaks the*
*skyline to the left, with the wooded slopes of the Claife*
*Heights to the right*

**British Library Cataloguing in Publication Data**

Smith, Roland *1944–*
    Walking the great views.
    1. Great Britain. Recreations. Walking
    I. Title
    796.510941

    ISBN 0-7153-9482-7

Text © Roland Smith, 1991
Photographs © John Cleare, 1991
Maps © Mark Richards, 1991

Typeset by Typesetters (Birmingham) Ltd
Smethwick, West Midlands
and printed in Hong Kong
by Wing King Tong Co Ltd
for David & Charles plc
Brunel House    Newton Abbot    Devon

# CONTENTS

## INTRODUCTION · 9

The Magnificent Seven | 16

## 1 THE ROOTS OF SCENERY · 21

Pre-Cambrian: | 21
    Beacon Hill, Charnwood Forest
A Route to Beacon Hill | 23
Millstone Grit: Brimham Rocks | 24
A Route to Brimham Rocks | 25
Limestone: Farleton Fell | 28
Limestone Scenery | 30
Whin Sill: High Cup Nick | 31
The Pennine Way | 32
Basalt: The Storr and The Quiraing, Skye | 35
Routes to The Storr and The Quiraing | 37
Sandstone: The Brecon Beacons | 40
A Route to Pen-y-Fan | 41
Symond's Yat | 42
Masters of the Air | 45
Chalk: The Dorset Coast | 48

## 2 FOLKLORE AND LEGEND · 52

Giant Hills | 53
The Wrekin | 54
A Route to the Wrekin | 56
The Stiperstones | 58
Devil Hills | 60
A Route to Cader Idris | 61
Cader Idris | 61
The Afanc of Glaslyn | 64
The Fairy Princess of Llyn-y-Fan-fach | 64

King Arthur's Last Stand: Bwlch-y-Saethau    65
Routes to Snowdon    68
Cadbury and Glastonbury Tor    72
Arthur's Seat    78
Edinburgh's Hills    78
A Route to Robin Hood's Stride    80
Robin Hood's Stride    81
The Witches of Pendle    81

## 3 MONARCHS OF ALL THEY SURVEYED · 87

Cissbury Ring    90
Hambledon Hill    91
A Route to Hambledon and Hod Hills    92
Hod Hill    96
Mither Tap, Bennachie    96
Traprain Law    102
A Route to Tre'r Ceiri    103
Tre'r Ceiri    103
Mam Tor    104
A Route to Mam Tor    106
Ingleborough    110
A Route to Ingleborough    111
The British Camp, Malvern Hills    112
The Malvern Ridge    114
Wandlebury    116
East Anglian Views    117

## 4 MONUMENTAL VIEWPOINTS · 119

Hadrian's Wall    121
A Walk Along the Wall    124
The Glenfinnan Monument    125
More Eyeful Towers    127
The Westbury White Horse    130
Views from the Battlefields    131
The Dassett Hills    134
Broadway Tower    135
The Cotswold Way    136
Greenwich Park    141
Cook Monument, Easby Moor    143
Managing the Moorlands    145
The Penshaw Monument    147
A Route to Penshaw Hill    148
McCaig's Folly    153
Mow Cop    153

## 5 LITERARY LANDSCAPES · 156

William Wordsworth: Lake District    156
A Wordsworth Walk    157
Beatrix Potter: Cat Bells    160
George Borrow: Snowdon    162
Borrow's Wild Wales    164
Sir Walter Scott: Eildon Hills    165
A Traverse of the Eildon Hills    166
R. D. Blackmore: Exmoor    170
A Route to the Doone Valley    172
Thomas Hardy's Wessex    173
A. E. Housman: Wenlock Edge    175
The Brontë Sisters: Haworth Moors    179
The Brontë Trail    180
Daniel Defoe: Blackstone Edge    183
A Route to Blackstone Edge    186

INDEX    188

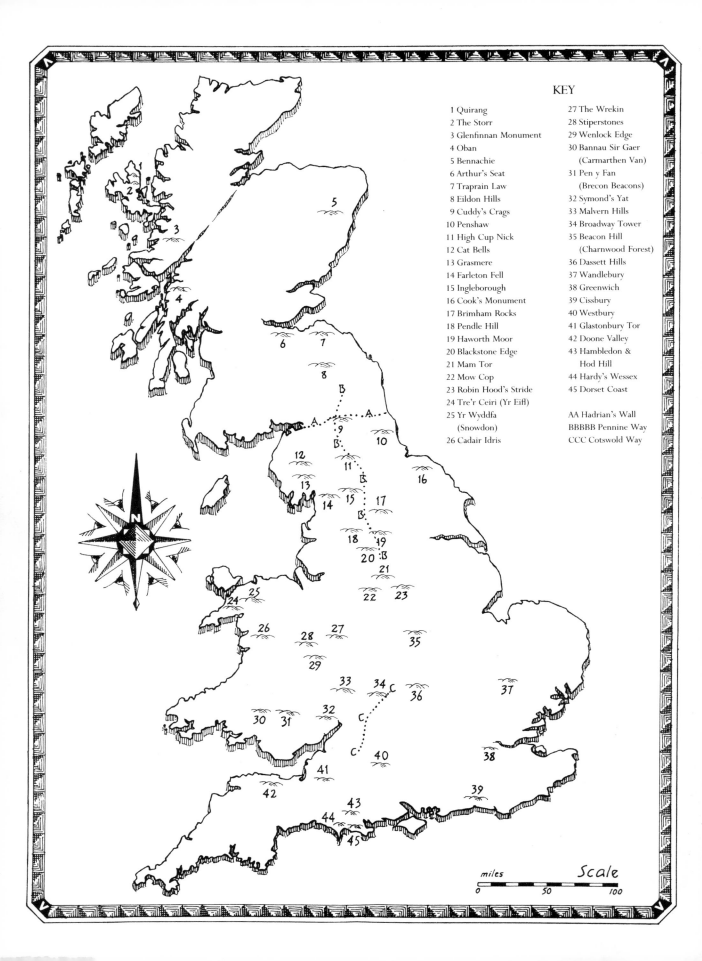

KEY

1 Quirang
2 The Storr
3 Glenfinnan Monument
4 Oban
5 Bennachie
6 Arthur's Seat
7 Traprain Law
8 Eildon Hills
9 Cuddy's Crags
10 Penshaw
11 High Cup Nick
12 Cat Bells
13 Grasmere
14 Farleton Fell
15 Ingleborough
16 Cook's Monument
17 Brimham Rocks
18 Pendle Hill
19 Haworth Moor
20 Blackstone Edge
21 Mam Tor
22 Mow Cop
23 Robin Hood's Stride
24 Tre'r Ceiri (Yr Eifl)
25 Yr Wyddfa
   (Snowdon)
26 Cadair Idris

27 The Wrekin
28 Stiperstones
29 Wenlock Edge
30 Bannau Sir Gaer
   (Carmarthen Van)
31 Pen y Fan
   (Brecon Beacons)
32 Symond's Yat
33 Malvern Hills
34 Broadway Tower
35 Beacon Hill
   (Charnwood Forest)
36 Dassett Hills
37 Wandlebury
38 Greenwich
39 Cissbury
40 Westbury
41 Glastonbury Tor
42 Doone Valley
43 Hambledon &
   Hod Hill
44 Hardy's Wessex
45 Dorset Coast

AA Hadrian's Wall
BBBBB Pennine Way
CCC Cotswold Way

miles
Scale
0        50        100

# INTRODUCTION:
## Roam with a View

Todd Crag is an insignificant, knobbly little Lakeland hill lying on the eastern shoulder of the more popular Loughrigg Fell at the northern end of Windermere, but it rears its craggy head over the tiny hamlet of Clappersgate on the Ambleside to Coniston road in a manner which belies its modest 212m (695ft).

Certainly, to a couple of likely lads on their first visit to the Lake District from their home in East Anglia, it was every inch a mountain. Driven early from their dripping tent after an uncomfortable night of driving rain, they glanced up at the glistening, beckoning crag as they drove over the Rothay Bridge just outside Ambleside. It was an invitation they just could not resist; after all, they had come to the Lakes to do some climbing, hadn't they? Without another word, they pulled up in the battered old Ford Popular by the telephone box at Clappersgate and set off on the narrow path up the hill through the rain-soaked trees and bracken.

It didn't take them long to reach the grey crag which guarded the summit, but they were somewhat taken aback to find it already occupied – by a goat. They struggled up the last 3m (10ft) of slimy, wet rock, their fashionable, winkle-picker shoes sliding uneasily in the greasy holds. At last they emerged on a small platform of bare rock, just as a weak, watery sun broke through the rolling grey clouds which had given them such an unpleasant night on the campsite.

Panting from their exertions, they clapped each other on the back: a summit at last! Even Hillary and Tensing could not have felt more relief and fulfilment than these two ill-equipped and novice 'mountaineers' from the flatlands of Essex. And what was revealed from that modest summit was to change the life of at least one of those climbers.

The stunning view from the top of Todd Crag took away what little breath the pair still had after their early morning scramble. The length of Windermere was revealed at a glance looking south, as the morning mist slowly dissolved under the heat of the newly emerged sun. Tiny yachts scudded about on the sparkling water, and a steamer chugged out from Ambleside pier beneath the wooded bulk of Wansfell Pike.

Looking north-east, the great swelling sepia fells of Red Screes and Caudale Head sheltered the gash of the Kirkstone Pass, but clouds hung menacingly over Fairfield, Dunmail Raise and the Langdale Pikes, with the Scafells, the highest land in England, still hidden under the threatening grey blanket. As the sun slowly and imperceptibly gained in strength, the clouds rolled back, unfolding more and more of the stupendous view. The two lads stood spellbound in the intoxicating air of that glorious autumnal morning. Quite simply, they had never seen anything more beautiful in their short lowland lives.

I was one of those climbers, and the memory of that magical September morning on Todd Crag was to instil in me a love of high country and walking just 'to see the view' which was to stay with me for the rest of my life. Higher summits in Wales, Scotland, the Alps and Iceland were later to beckon with the same irresistible magnetism, but modest little Todd Crag (from which, I was gratified to learn some years later, even the great Wainwright considered the view of Windermere 'striking') began it all.

The point about the great viewpoints is that usually they have very little to do with altitude. It is much more to do with the subtle relationships between landscape and landform, human history and the hoary hearsay of myth and legend.

More people enjoy Britain's countryside today

than ever before. According to the Countryside Commission, up to 18 million trips are now made to the countryside on a typical summer Sunday. And nearly 20 per cent of these trips include a walk of 2 miles (3km) or more – that's 3.6 million walking trips on a typical summer Sunday. The commission estimates that in 1988, 230 million walking trips of more than 2 miles were made to our countryside. With an unparalleled network of 140,000 miles (225,000km) of public rights of way in England and Wales, access to the countryside is easy, if not always unobstructed. With more people out walking than are involved in all the other outdoor sports and recreations put together, the question has to be asked, why do they walk? Again according to the Countryside Commission, the government's countryside watchdog,

*At 294m (965ft) Leith Hill is the culminating point of the long greensand ridge of the North Downs, and the highest point in south-east England. But until Bristol merchant Richard Hull built his 19.5m (64ft) tower in 1766, it didn't top the magic 1,000ft mark. Now it does, and the views from the Gothic tower encompass thirteen counties, from the dome of St Paul's Cathedral in London to the English Channel beyond the South Downs*

the reasons are not hard to find. It is because most people have a deep love and respect for the countryside, valuing it for its peace and tranquillity and for the opportunities it gives to enjoy fine scenery and healthy exercise.

And where are the best places to see the finest countryside? From those special viewpoints, of course, because I believe that most people, like me, walk purely and simply for the views.

The first stirrings of appreciation of fine scenery in this country are usually attributed to the eighteenth-century Romantics, with the Lakeland poets led by William Wordsworth in the forefront. Although he wrote 'Earth has not anything to show more fair' in praise of the view from Westminster Bridge in the heart of London, Wordsworth is better known for introducing the delectable Lake District to thousands of tourists. It was he who, in his 1810 'Description of the Scenery of the Lakes in the North of England', wrote: 'I do not know any tract of country in which, in so narrow a compass, may be found an equal variety in the influences of light and shadow upon the substance and beautiful features of the landscape.' He could have been describing that view from Todd Crag.

Followers of the Lakeland 'Grand Tour' often

viewed the scenery with the aid of a Claude glass, which reversed, miniaturised and tinted the view in an attempt to make it even more 'picturesque' – that is, like a picture. But earlier travellers, like the intrepid Celia Fiennes who travelled alone and on side-saddle through Britain in the late seventeenth century, and the cynical journalist Daniel Defoe a few years later, saw only horrors and 'howling wildernesses' in the hills, and usually did not even stop to admire the view.

However, the love of the countryside and the joy of admiring it from high places goes back much further, at least as far as William Langland's fourteenth-century masterpiece *The Vision Concerning Piers the Ploughman* and that 'faire felde of folk' he observed from the crest of the Malvern Hills one bright medieval May morning.

Indeed, it is hard not to believe that prehistoric man also shared the same love of high places when you look at the siting of his most important monuments. Most prominent among these in Britain are the three thousand or so hillforts, mainly dating from the Iron Age, which ring so many of our most commanding heights. Arch-

*Walkers cluster around the summit cairn of Yr Wyddfa, the summit of Snowdon, in this view from the summit ridge to the east. Beneath the reigning peak are the waters of Llyn Llydaw and the distant Moel Siabod*

aeologists now believe that many of these so-called hillforts were by no means purely defensive or military in their use and purpose. Most seem to have been inhabited, either permanently or seasonally, by peaceful farming communities. They may have been small tribal villages, trading centres, or even family farms comparable with the moated enclosures of the Middle Ages. Or they may merely have been summer shielings, from where grazing animals could be watched over a wide distance.

Our ancestors not only liked to live in high places, but they also revered them to the extent that they chose the highest points as burial places for their dead leaders. The whole of upland Britain is dotted with tumuli where important local chieftains were interred, perhaps to be nearer to their gods, or maybe to continue to watch over those left behind.

PEN-Y-GADER-FAWR _____

*The view north-east towards Hay Bluff and the Wye Valley from Twmpa, on the northern escarpment of the Black Mountains. Pen-y-Gader-fawr lies three miles due south, above the plantations of the Mynydd Ddu ('Black Mountains') Forest*

SCAFELL ──────────────

*The highest land in England. The Scafell massif, with Scafell 964m (3,162ft) in the centre, and Scafell Pike 978m (3,210ft) on the left, across the green enclosed meadows of Wasdale Head from the neighbouring peak of Yewbarrow*

# THE MAGNIFICENT SEVEN

Some interesting research has been done on the question of exactly how far you can see from the high points in this country. This led my good friend, Manchester journalist Tom Waghorn, to the calculation that, under perfect conditions, you could scan the entire length of Britain in seven great eyefuls.

The late Arnold Whipp, of Whitefield, Manchester, had been much exercised with the question of long-distance view-points, and he compiled an extensive list of the longest recorded views in Britain. Many of them were over 50 miles (80km) and the greatest over 150 miles (241km) – for example, the view of the Wicklow Mountains of southern Ireland from Coniston Old Man in the Lake District, and the Southern Uplands of Scotland from the summit of Snowdon. The limits of the distance the viewer can see obviously varies with the weather conditions and the altitude of the spectator. On the level, a 1.5m (5ft) tall person should be able to see a distance of nearly 3 miles (5km). At 150m (500ft) Mr Whipp calculated that in good conditions, the viewer should be able to see 29.5 miles (47.4km); while at 300m (1,000ft), the distance increased to 41.6 miles (66.9km). At 910m (3,000ft), taking refraction of the atmosphere into account, you should be able to see an astonishing 72 miles (115.8km).

The 'Magnificent Seven' viewpoints, according to Mr Whipp's tables, were: Leith Hill, Surrey to Whitehorse Hill, Oxfordshire; Whitehorse Hill to Pen-y-Gader-fawr, in the Black Mountains; Pen-y-Gader-fawr to Snowdon; Snowdon to Scafell, Cumbria; Scafell to The Merrick, Galloway; The Merrick to Ben More, Isle of Mull, and Ben More to Beinn Mhor on South Uist, in the Outer Hebrides.

*A view of The Merrick, at 842m (2,764ft), the highest point in southern Scotland, from near the Devil's Bowling Green on the boulder-strewn granite north ridge of Craignaw 645m (2,116ft) in Galloway's Range of the Awful Hand. The Merrick rises to the left, with Kirriereoch Hill, Tarfessock, and Shallock on Minnoch to the right*

Our fertile folklore has always inhabited the hills and high places of Britain with supernatural beings, and many of our most famous viewpoints are associated with giants or legendary heroes, such as King Arthur or Robin Hood. The study of an Ordnance Survey map of almost any part of Britain from Cornwall to Caithness, while always an enlightening experience, will also more often than not produce one or two of these famous names. The fact is that both King Arthur and Robin Hood were universal folk heroes and probably always existed more in the minds of men than in historical fact.

Echoing the sentiments of their ancient forebears, the sometimes eccentric landed gentry of more recent times often constructed their follies and landmarks on the highest points of their estates because of the view and the fact that they could be seen for miles around. Exactly the same criteria dictated the original sitings of the ancient white horses and other monuments on the chalk downs of southern Britain.

Having already said that the prerequisite of the finest viewpoints is not always altitude, it must be added that to enjoy most of them will involve some climbing, and many are in the hills. So a word about mountain safety and navigation in the hills is important.

The mountains of Britain, modest as they are, can be killers unless they are treated with respect. But as a long-serving member of the mountain rescue service has said: 'It's not the hills that are dangerous; it's the people who use them.' As long as you take sensible precautions, which will include being properly equipped for unpredictable weather, wearing adequate footwear, and carrying a map and a compass and knowing how to use them, you should come to no harm. A great deal of nonsense is written about walking equipment, but all that is necessary is that you should keep warm and dry. Professionals like shepherds and gamekeepers, who spend most of their lives working on the hills, seem to survive wearing a good tweed jacket, trousers and a macintosh, and the earliest Everest climbers went to well over 6,000m (20,000ft) in similar clothing. You can spend as much as you like on expensive, hi-tech 'breathable' fabrics, and they *are* excellent, but don't think that you cannot venture out into the

*A winter evening's view of snow-capped Ben More 966m (3,169ft) seen from the north-west over Loch Tuath near Fanmore, on the Inner Hebridean island of Mull*

hills unless and until you have all the latest gear.

Map-reading is important, and there is no substitute for the 1:25,000 Ordnance Survey Pathfinder series for the serious walker. The 1:50,000 Landranger series is useful for locating your viewpoint and putting it in context. Fortunately, many of the more popular walking areas are now covered by the excellent 1:25,000 Outdoor Leisure series on which viewpoints are normally shown by a blue sunset symbol. They also appear on the 1:50,000 Tourist or Landranger series in red, but be warned, some of the viewpoints appear to have been inserted with little or no local knowledge and merely a cursory look for high points. I well remember an asterisk-style vantage point symbol which was inserted on the summit of Kinder Scout on the old Dark Peak Outdoor

OVERLEAF

*One man and his dog on the long south-east ridge of Beinn Mhor, on the Outer Hebridean island of South Uist. Looking south over island-dotted Loch Eynort towards the distant hills of Barra*

Leisure sheet. A less inspiring viewpoint would be hard to find.

Not only is a map essential in the field, but there are few more pleasurable activities for long winter evenings than to plan your next expedition to that sought-after view, or to remember and relive your last trip. With just a little practice, a good map can be read and reread a thousand times, giving the reader far greater pleasure and information than any book.

Of course, any personal list of favourite viewpoints is bound to be subjective, and some people might even conceivably enjoy the view from the bottom of a peat grough on Kinder. So, I am *not* suggesting that these views are definitively *the* best, most extensive and interesting. What follows, therefore, is a personal excursion around some *favourite* viewpoints in England, Scotland and Wales. Each chapter looks at viewpoints thematically, taking the subjects of geology and geomorphology; folklore and legend; prehistory; monuments and follies, and landscapes which have inspired great literature, as the main headings. Many of the subjects inevitably overlap, for our landscape is a living record which has been written on over and over again – for example, Cadbury Castle in Somerset, as well as being associated with King Arthur and Camelot, is also a classic Iron Age hillfort, and the Wandlebury hillfort outside Cambridge also apparently had figures carved in the chalk hillside on its ramparts.

In each case, the stories behind the viewpoints are explored, and brief descriptions and sketch maps of walks to some of the viewpoints are given. This book has not been designed for use in the field as a walking guide; the descriptions are merely 'tasters' to encourage you to explore the area for yourself and to discover your own routes. To assist the avid viewfinder, there are grid references and map details at the end of each chapter. The location of the major viewpoints is shown on the UK map.

As already explained, the featured viewpoints are the individual choices of the author and photographer which have been selected from personal experience, knowledge and enthusiasm. I apologise in advance if you do not find your favourite here. The final selection was exceedingly difficult and many firm favourites were omitted in the interests of having a representative selection. Examples of these are Win Hill, perhaps the finest viewpoint in the Peak; Wastwater from Westmorland Crags on Great Gable, and the aerial view of Holy Island and Brodick Bay from Goat Fell on the Isle of Arran. What is left is a walker's personal viewfinder of Britain. I hope it will encourage you to go out and 'roam with a view', opening your eyes to some of the most beautiful and interesting landscapes in the world.

---

FACTBOX KEY

GR: Grid Reference

OL: Outdoor Leisure Ordnance Survey Map

LR: Landranger Ordnance Survey Map

---

FACTBOX

| | GR | MAP |
|---|---|---|
| Todd Crag, Cumbria | NY362039 | OL7 English Lakes – S.E. Sheet |
| Leith Hill, Surrey | TQ135434 | LR187, Dorking, Reigate & Crawley |
| Whitehorse Hill, Oxfordshire | SU303868 | LR174 Newbury & Wantage |
| Pen-y-Gader-fawr, Black Mountains | SO229288 | LR161 Abergavenny & Black Mountains |
| Snowdon, Gwynedd | SH610544 | OL17 Snowdonia – Snowdon |
| Scafell, Cumbria | NY207067 | LR89/90 West Cumbria/Penrith |
| The Merrick, Galloway | NX415851 | LR77 Dalmellington |
| Ben More, Mull | NM525331 | LR47/48 Tobermory & Mull |
| Beinn Mhor, South Uist | NF808312 | LR22 Benbecula |

# 1
# THE ROOTS
# OF SCENERY

The countryside of Britain is a palimpsest on which many stories have been written and rewritten during the ten thousand years of human history. But the parchment on which those stories are written goes back even further in the almost unimaginably ancient geological timescale, perhaps as much as one thousand million years. For such a small island, Britain is richly endowed with a geology in which all the great systems of the world are represented. Even the names given to the classic periods of the geological eras are reminders of the pioneering work of British scientists in the field.

The earliest eras of Cambrian and pre-Cambrian take their name from Cambria, or Wales; while the Ordovician and Silurian periods of the Palaeozoic era are named after two tribes of Celtic Britons who lived in the wild Welsh borderlands where the rocks are particularly well exposed and where they were first described. The rich red sandstone of the Devonian period takes its name from the West-country county where the underlying rocks colour the very soil; while the limestones, gritstones and coal measures and chalks of the Carboniferous and Cretaceous periods are both descriptive of the British conditions which existed respectively some three hundred million and one hundred million years ago.

The following walks and viewpoints are intended to show the richness of our geological heritage and the way in which the underlying rocks have shaped the landscapes which we admire today. Not every period is represented, of course, but most of the major eras will be described by relating them to the landforms which they typically have created.

## PRE-CAMBRIAN:
## BEACON HILL, CHARNWOOD FOREST

The earliest rocks now exposed in Britain are also among the oldest in the world. Geologists call these complex-structured rocks 'pre-Cambrian' because they pre-date the earliest stratified rocks of the Cambrian era and originate from the very genesis of planet Earth. Pre-Cambrian rocks outcrop rarely in Britain, appearing most notably in the north-west Highlands of Scotland, on the Pembrokeshire coast and the Anglesey cliffs of Wales, at Ingleton in the Yorkshire Dales, on the Long Mynd in Shropshire, and in the Malvern Hills of Hereford and Worcester.

There is another site of pre-Cambrian rocks, however, which should be familiar to the thousands of motorists who use the M1 motorway as they speed north from the capital. As the motorway winds north of Leicester between junctions 22 and 23 it climbs through what remains of the ancient Charnwood Forest, a former hunting ground of kings and princes and recently short-listed with neighbouring Need-wood as the site for a new national forest. As the road gains height, it passes through shallow cuttings in which the pale, pastel colours of the slaty, pre-Cambrian bedrocks are exposed on either side, and the livid scar of an active quarry is revealed on the left among a group of pines. Bradgate Park is a 323ha (800 acre) playground for the city of Leicester, gifted to its citizens by wealthy local industrialist Charles Bennion in 1928, with the instruction that it was for 'the quiet enjoyment of the people for all time'. Thousands of local people have been grateful for that act of benefaction, and have come to value the moorland, ancient pollarded woods and lakes

## A ROUTE TO BEACON HILL

Park in Bradgate Park Country Park near the Cropston Reservoir. Before setting off for Beacon Hill, it is worth exploring the old deer park with its pollarded oaks and the romantic ruins of Bradgate House and Old John's Tower. The park was given to the citizens of Leicester by industrialist Charles Bennion. Head due north on the road which follows the western shore of the reservoir and take the field path which leads into Swithland Wood, a remnant of the ancient Charnwood Forest, with old slate pits and quarries hidden deep among the venerable oaks. Please take care near these dangerous flooded pits. Still heading north, pass through the hamlet known as The Brands and enter the village of Woodhouse Eaves by the Swithland Road. Here the Wheatsheaf Inn offers a convenient refreshment stop.

Descending a steep hill from the village on a field path, you cross the Woodhouse Road and enter the Beacon Hill Country Park, with its jagged outcrops and fine views. There are many paths around the prominent Beacon for children to explore. If you do not wish to retrace your steps, an alternative route back to your car and Bradgate Park is provided by field paths which pass through Broombriggs Farm, east of Woodhouse Eaves, then by crossing a golf course and passing between Ling Hill to the west and wooded Warren Hill to the east to reach the park. You will re-enter Bradgate Park at its north-west corner, beneath Old John's Tower, from where it is a mile back through the deer-haunted parkland to your car.

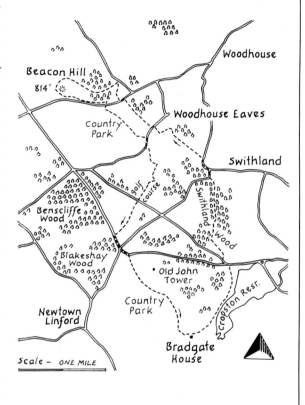

Twisted and tortured pre-Cambrian rocks outcrop above the oatgrass, bracken and rosebay willow herb which ring the summit of Beacon Hill, in Leicestershire's Charnwood Forest. These ancient rocks – among the oldest in Britain – owe their contortions to their origin in a violent past. They were spewed out by ancient volcanoes which erupted perhaps 700 million years ago. Later earth movements compacted and crushed these lavas to form the hard, erosion-resistant rocks we see today. The incredibly hard slates and crystalline rocks of Charnwood have been extensively quarried over the years, as is evidenced in the local landscape

of the park as a vital escape from the hosiery and footwear factories which were the basis of Leicester's modern fortune.

Our first walk starts in Bradgate Park, where red and fallow deer still graze in what are the remains of the medieval Charnwood Forest. The gorge of the Linford Brook, which is such a pleasant feature of the park, was formed when the stream cut through the hard pre-Cambrian rocks which ring the forest as it made its way to the softer surrounding marls. In the heart of the park near Cropston Reservoir are the ruins of Bradgate House, built as a hunting lodge by Thomas Grey, the 1st Marquis of Dorset, in 1490. Little remains of the house today except for the chapel, but it was one of the first English country houses to be built in brick primarily as an unfortified residence. On the 213m (700ft) hill above the house, the folly known as Old John commemorates a retainer of the 5th Earl of Stamford who was killed, apparently, by a falling tree. It bears a striking resemblance to the Mow Cop folly we shall meet later in Chapter 4.

But undoubtedly the most famous resident of Bradgate Park was Lady Jane Grey, the tragic and uncrowned 'Queen for Nine Days' following the death of King Edward VI in 1553. Sixteen-year-old Jane was placed on the throne by her scheming father-in-law, the Duke of Northumberland, only to be executed the following year by order of Mary Tudor, who eventually succeeded her.

Walking north and following the road which runs alongside the western shore of Cropston Reservoir, field paths lead to the ancient deciduous woodland of Swithland Wood. There are a number of old slate pits and quarries hidden deep in the pollarded oaks and birches of the wood, from which an attractive blue-green slate used locally for roofing and tombstones was quarried from medieval times, before thinner Welsh slates were introduced. The main quarry is now flooded and its margins have become overgrown as nature reclaims this site of former industry. The sheer walls of steeply dipping rock are reflected in the deep still waters, and the perimeter fence should not be ignored by the curious visitor – such pools can be dangerous.

In some of the overgrown quarries of Swithland Wood the younger sandstones which later ages deposited over the pre-Cambrian bedrock can still be seen, deposited in hollows in the older rock. Gradually and imperceptibly, more of the ancient pre-Cambrian landscape is revealed. As you enter the village of Woodhouse Eaves via the Swithland Road, make for the Beacon Hill Country Park, where the summit provides one of the best viewpoints in the East Midlands. The faint earthworks which surround the bare 248m (813ft) summit of Beacon Hill are all that remains of an Iron Age hillfort, where excavations have revealed even earlier occupation, dating from the Bronze Age. There is a useful toposcope about

90m to the east of the summit which indicates, among other things, the 45m (150ft) bell tower in Queen's Park, Loughborough, 3 miles (5km) to the north-east, and the M1 which cuts an ugly, constantly buzzing swathe across the countryside due west.

Those ancient pre-Cambrian rocks outcrop again on the wind-swept but seldom lonely, bracken-ringed summit, and the lush, wooded landscape spreading below gives a bird's eye view of the fertile hunting shire of Leicestershire. This is Quorn country, and the neatly hedged and spinneyed countryside provides some of the finest fox-hunting in Britain. Whatever your views on the morality of hunting, if you appreciate the fine typically English patchwork-quilt landscape revealed from Beacon Hill, you should realise that it owes everything to the requirements of the fox-hunting fraternity. The copses, spinneys and coverts which occupy the corners of so many of the square Enclosure Act fields are provided almost exclusively for the benefit of Reynard and the pleasure of those whom Oscar Wilde described as 'the unspeakable in pursuit of the uneatable'.

You can spend a fruitful hour or so exploring the many nooks and crannies of Beacon Hill and its environs, where a whole succession of crystalline rocks from the very basement of our geology are exposed, poking through the more recent clays, marls and sandstones. The children will love this mini mountain range.

### MILLSTONE GRIT: BRIMHAM ROCKS

Another view point of geological interest which is always a great favourite with children is the weird millstone grit outcrop of Brimham Rocks, 3 miles (5km) east of Pateley Bridge in beautiful Nidderdale on the edge of the Yorkshire Dales. Once described by an over-enthusiastic devotee as 'the world's most interesting collection of rocks', Brimham could justifiably lay claim to be the most fascinating rock garden in Britain. As an example of the artistic powers of the natural forces of erosion on the apparently hard, unyielding gritstone, it is unrivalled in Britain. Only the granite tors of Dartmoor and the similarly formed gritstone tors of the Peak can remotely match Brimham's magic rock garden.

# A Route to Brimham Rocks

Silhouetted against the sky, a pair of rock climbers get to grips with one of Brimham's most famous outcrops, the Dancing Bear. The short but often severe climbs on Brimham's coarse gritstone present an interesting challenge to climbers in an unusual, if often crowded, situation. Climbing began here over a century ago, but until the 1950s the area was rarely visited except by local climbers, notably from the Harrogate area. Today's gritstone tigers can often be seen testing their skills on the rough but tactile rock. The hardest climbs are found along the edge to the west of the House.

The large National Trust car park to the south of the rocks is the one most tourists use if they are visiting this extraordinary collection of gritstone tors. But a more pleasant 4–5 mile (6–8km) ramble which puts the rocks in their proper perspective in the Nidderdale scene starts from Brimham Hall, 2 miles (3km) up a minor road from the hamlet of Burnt Yates, which is on the main valley road, the B6165.

Walk up this road almost to its end, leaving it for the bridleway signposted 'Brimham and Warsil' where it turns sharply to the left. On the right of this track is the ancient Monk Wall, associated with the extensive sheep and cattle-rearing properties of the Cistercian monks of nearby Fountains Abbey. Looking over the wall, there are extensive views towards How Hill, which shelters the famous abbey, and across the Vale of Mowbray. Riva Hill is prominent on the left. At a cattle grid, follow the road to the left and for the first time you will notice the weird outcrops of Brimham on the skyline ahead.

Turn right at the first road junction and drop down to the trees alongside Thornton Beck on a concrete track. Turn left in the trees on a green track which crosses the stream just past Summer Wood House. Eventually, you emerge near the most north-easterly of the outcrops of Brimham, known as Hare Heads.

You now wend your way south through the heather to this fantastic rock garden of natural architecture, but allow a good hour to explore properly every nook and cranny of Brimham Rocks. There are surprises around every corner. Leaving the rocks by the main entrance on the road up from Summerbridge, take the well-defined track along the ridge opposite. The track goes across gorse-dotted Graffa Plain and to the right of Riva Hill, with Riva Hill Farm to the left. Reaching the concrete track again, turn right opposite the road to Riva Hill Farm, ascending a hill on the footpath with fine views of Nidderdale ahead, then descending to Shepherd's Lodge Farm and eventually back to the Monk Wall track and your car.

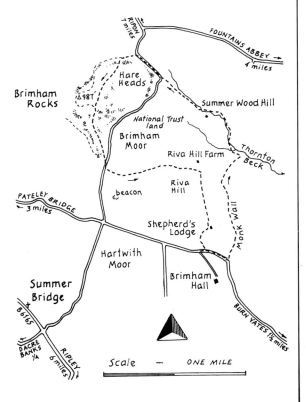

Such was the awe in which these strangely shaped rocks were held in the past that until comparatively recently they were regarded as man-made. Over-active Victorian imaginations conveniently linked them to the activities of the ever-mysterious Druids, a notion which is reflected in some of the names of the rock formations, such as the Druid's Idol, the Druid's Writing Desk and the Druid's Coffin. The idea that white-robed and bearded Druids were responsible for the construction of Brimham Rocks seems to have emanated from a paper presented by the antiquarian excavator Major Rooke to the Antiquarian Society in 1786. In it, Rooke stated that the rocks seemed to have been built 'by artists skilled in the power of mathematics'. Even some of today's visitors find it hard to believe that these fantastic formations are completely natural. During Queen Victoria's reign, the number of visitors to Brimham Rocks by wagonette and dog cart increased rapidly, and in 1885, three thousand people attended a Wesleyan rally, complete with brass band and a choir of one hundred.

The National Trust accepted the 146ha (362 acres) of the Brimham Rocks Estate in 1970 and immediately began a programme of conservation that was designed to protect this unique landscape for future generations. Until then, car parking was uncontrolled and random among the rock formations. Now large car parks are provided to the south of the main outcrops, which are reached by an easy walk on good paths through the heather. The best plan for a short visit is to walk towards Brimham House, now the National Trust office and information centre, and wander beyond it to the northernmost formations, including the Druid's Idol, a massive, 200 ton rock precariously perched on a pedestal only 30cm (12in) in diameter. Turn south to explore the other fantastic rocks which form the centre and the western perimeter of the moor, from the life-like Dancing Bear to the Cannon, the Watchdog and the Sphinx. The White Rocking Stone, high on the southern range of crags, was once white-washed and apparently visible from Harrogate, nearly 10 miles (16km) away.

Longer walks, which put the rocks in their proper perspective to the rest of Nidderdale, include the walk up from Pateley Bridge across

Pateley Moor and Low Bishopside; or from Ripley via Thornton Beck or Graffa Plain, a 4½ mile (7km) ramble which crosses the Monk Wall, a reminder of the days when Brimham Rocks were grazed by the sheep and cattle of the Cistercian monks of nearby Fountains Abbey.

One of my best memories of Brimham was a delightful family picnic we enjoyed while on holiday at Summerbridge. We feasted on delicious purple bilberries (a Brimham speciality) and ice cream as we sat on the flat top of Lover's Leap, with the whole of Nidderdale, as far as the grim heights of Great Whernside, spread out before us. On that glorious September day we really did feel masters of all we surveyed.

To learn how the fantastic rock artistry of Brimham evolved, we must go back three hundred million years to the Carboniferous period, when gritty sands were deposited in the delta of an enormous river which flooded down from a mountain range in the north. Buried under later deposits of rock, these sands were compressed to form the millstone grit, and later exposed by uplift and erosion to stand on the surface again. The finishing touches, of which Henry Moore would surely be proud, were achieved by the timeless and persistent erosive forces of ice, rain and wind, which ate away at weaker joints to create the natural sculpture park that is Brimham today.

*The Druid's Writing Desk, Brimham Rocks, is just one among an amazing collection of natural rock sculptures which cover the gritstone plateau three miles east of Pateley Bridge in Nidderdale. The connection of these weird gritstone tors with the Druids stems from the imagination of eighteenth-century antiquaries, who could not believe these strange shapes could possibly have a natural origin. In addition to the Druid's Writing Desk, on the northernmost edge of the moor overlooking the enclosed farmland of Pateley Moor towards Upper Nidderdale, Brimham boasts a Druid's Idol, a Druid's Coffin and a Druid's Cave. It is interesting to note how more modern visitors have invented contemporary nicknames such as General de Gaulle and Donald Duck*

### LIMESTONE: FARLETON FELL

Limestone is another member of the Carboniferous family of rocks, and it, too, can create some truly incredible landforms and viewpoints. Formed of the fossils of countless millions of tiny sea creatures which lived in a shallow tropical sea which extended over much of the British Isles some three hundred million years ago, our Carboniferous or Mountain Limestones have left us some of our most spectacular landscapes. The most famous examples are those in the Yorkshire Dales, where features like Malham Cove, Gordale Scar and Kilnsey Crag have attracted artists and

students for years. This is classic 'glacio-karst' scenery – a limestone landscape sculpted by ice – which is well known for its features of limestone pavements, scars and screes.

But my favourite area of limestone is an insignificant little hill mid-way between the Lakes and the Dales which has been the scene of some of the happiest family holidays we have had. As you approach Lancaster on the M6, with the pepper-pot tower of the Ashton Memorial prominent, the hills close in, forcing the motorway towards the shifting sands of Morecambe Bay. Around Junction 36, the motorway threads through a belt of Carboniferous limestone, and

*A stunted hawthorn, bent by the prevailing winds, somehow survives on the clints and grikes of the extensive limestone pavement above Newbiggin Crags, west of Farleton Fell. This is a limestone-lover's paradise with acres of fretted, geometrical landscape*

the great grey terraced bulk of Farleton Fell, 'the Gibraltar of Westmorland', appears on the right, with the extensive limestone pavements of Hutton Roof beyond. This is a hidden gem of limestone scenery and, incidentally, is one of the best viewpoints in the north of England, according to a distinguished mountaineering author who lives nearby.

Like a well-mannered courtesan, Farleton Fell hides its charms from the view of the *hoi polloi* speeding north towards the better known and certainly more crowded destinations in the Lake District or Scotland. But for those who know it, Farleton offers a peace and solitude which is rare nowadays among our hills. The best approach to Farleton Fell is from the village from which it takes its name. Turning off the A6070, which used to be the main highway to Scotland before the advent of the A6 and the M6, you take the signposted footpath by the side of a whitewashed cottage. When you reach the gate in the top left-hand corner of the field, turn left to skirt a small spinney of trees which shields a small limestone quarry. This fed the lime kiln which is marked by an obelisk in the meadow below. The quicklime was transported to the industrial towns of Lancashire by a quay on the Preston to Lancaster Canal, opened in 1819, which forms a prominent foreground feature in the ever-expanding views from the fell. Your gradually ascending route takes you past several other small abandoned quarries in the gorse and bracken of the hillside. Eventually, the path drops down to a hedge which meets the Jubilee Track, constructed to build the beacon which celebrated Queen Victoria's Jubilee in 1897. This leads easily up through clumps of gorse where linnets chitter their melodic song and buzzards soar with the hang-gliders overhead. As the track gradually turns east for the final ascent, the view opens up to the north to the seductively smooth outlines of the Howgills and the distinctive, flat-topped shape of Ingleborough appears ahead.

Now you enter a broad dry valley, rimmed by the crags which mark the edge of the extensive area of limestone pavement and which also guard the summit of the fell. How you reach the 265m (870ft) rocky summit of Farleton Fell is a matter of personal choice. You can either thread your way through the modest crags on the left which bring you out on top of the pavement, or you can walk straight ahead towards the gap on the skyline which reveals a spectacular view south across the great 'wet Sahara' of Morecambe Bay, before turning left to reach the ladder stile which gives access to the top.

On a clear day the view from here is truly

# LIMESTONE SCENERY

All rocks exert a powerful influence on the landscape, but perhaps none is more distinctive and powerful than limestone. Limestone is the only common rock which is physically strong, yet will also dissolve in rainwater. Thus landscape which is literally as hard as rock can be shaped by the gentle force of a raindrop. As rainwater falls, it becomes slightly acidic by absorbing carbon dioxode from the air and the soil. The acidic water seeps through the limestone, slowly widening cracks by solution, and eventually opening up stream passages and cave systems.

Limestone landscapes formed by these strong but subtle forces are known as 'karst', a name which comes from a famous limestone area in Yugoslavia. The best limestone scenery in Britain is found in the Yorkshire Dales, the Peak District, the Mendips south of Bristol, and in South Wales. A common feature of karst scenery are the crags, or 'scars', of bare, dazzlingly white limestone on valley sides, often with extensive fans of scree at their foot. Dry valleys and gorges are often the most exciting features of a karst landscape, and classic examples include Malham Cove and Gordale Scar in the Yorkshire Dales, the Winnats Pass and Cave Dale in the Peak, and Cheddar Gorge in the Mendips. These now usually dry features were cut by abrasive meltwater torrents from the retreating glaciers at the end of the Ice Age flowing across the still-frozen ground.

Limestone scenery also creates its own flora, and the 'clints' (blocks) and 'grikes' (cracks) in the rocks of limestone pavements, scraped clean by the ice, such as those on Farleton Fell, support a varied and colourful plant life.

But perhaps the most famous features of the limestone landscape are the caves and caverns that were formed by the dissolving power of the slightly acidic rainwater. This is the world of the caver or potholer, the follower of an esoteric sport which demands bravery, the right equipment, and above all, experience. But the unique underground scenery of limestone country is also open to lesser mortals because many of the most spectacular caverns are open to the public, well-lit and interpreted so that anyone can enjoy them.

*A view from inside the impressive confines of the gorge of Gordale Scar, near Malham in the Yorkshire Dales. The 50m (300ft) walls of limestone, initially formed by the Middle Craven Fault, rise dramatically above the crystal waters of Gordale Beck. The gorge is thought to have been deepened by the powerful meltwaters of Ice Age glaciers flowing off the limestone plateau above. Gordale and neighbouring Malham Cove are both classic examples of glacio-karst limestone scenery, justly popular for school geography field-trips*

magnificent. The treacherous sands of Morecambe Bay glisten beyond Arnside Knott, with the central fells of Lakeland, the Langdale Pikes, prominent, forming the backdrop. Looking south, you can see as far as the Ashton Memorial at Lancaster, with the M6 snaking towards it. North, the motorway, looking insignificant at this height, leads the eye unerringly across the drumlins of the Kent Valley to the noble Howgill Fells, while, turning east, Ingleborough and the heights of Three Peak Country stand proud. Nearer to hand, the clints and grikes of the limestone pavement, formed by the slightly corrosive action of rainfall on the calcium carbonate of the rock, make for a fascinating study. Their deep damp crevices are home to a marvellous variety of lime-loving plants, such as hart's tongue fern, dog's mercury and the lovely delicate red stars of herb robert.

Picking your way carefully east across the gently angled pavement, you come to a delightful little boulder-strewn dell where wind-stunted and sheep-cropped hawthorns, junipers and yews make a wonderful adventure playground for imaginative children – and for childish adults, too. Depending on time, you can extend your exploration of this enchanted landscape by walking east across Newbiggin Crags, crossing a minor road to the even bigger pavements of Hutton Roof, with its intriguing names like the Blasterfoot Gap, Potslacks, Uberash Plain and the delightfully descriptive Ploverlands. But beware, it is easy to lose your way and all sense of time in this bewitching sea of limestone crags and pavements.

## WHIN SILL: HIGH CUP NICK

A few miles further north the M6 passes through surely the most spectacular section on any British motorway at the Lune Gorge, with its close-up views of the smoothly rounded Silurian slates of the Howgills. Descending from the wastes of Shap, the observant motorist may pick out, across the valley of the Eden to the east, the dim blue outline of the highest points in the Pennines. These 'East of Eden' heights are our next objective, and we will be heading for a spot which has been described as 'one of Britain's greatest geomorphologic landmarks', and which is

featured in almost every geography textbook. High Cup Nick is one of the great moments on Tom Stephenson's classic route up the backbone of England – the Pennine Way. It literally bursts on the senses of the weary wayfarer who has plodded through peat bog and heather for 158 miles (254km) from Edale.

After the long haul across the featureless wastes of the falsely named Golden Mea from Cauldron Snout, the Way enters the pleasant limestone pastures of Maize Beck before emerging onto the limestone-pavement-dotted expanse of High Cup Plain.

*(continued on p34)*

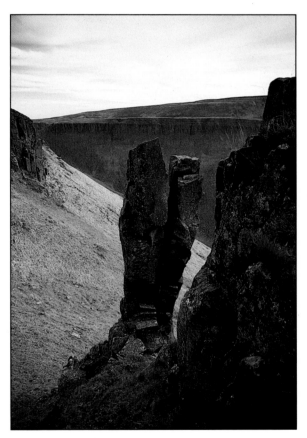

*The pinnacle of Nichol Chair, or Last, is among the dolerite crags which rim the impressive amphitheatre of High Cup Nick. Said to have been named after a local Dufton cobbler who climbed up and soled a pair of boots on its miniscule summit, Nichol Chair is just one of several tottering pinnacles of the Great Whin Sill rock which ring the Nick. This view looks east towards High Cupgill Head, with High Cup Scar and Murton Fell beyond*

# THE PENNINE WAY

It took Tom Stephenson, campaigning outdoor journalist and life-long fighter for access, thirty years to set up Britain's best-known and toughest long-distance footpath – the Pennine Way. And the 250 mile (400km) route, which snakes up the backbone of England, remains his lasting memorial and the ultimate challenge and yardstick to the British backpacker. Usually accomplished from south to north, from the green valley of Edale in the Peak District to the gypsy capital of Kirk Yetholm just across the Scottish border, the Pennine Way, like so many of our designated long-distance routes, has become a victim of its own popularity. Erosion, caused by tens of thousands of walkers' boots, has created ugly scars on many sections, particularly on the first section across Kinder Scout and Bleaklow in the Peak, and on Pen-y-ghent in Yorkshire.

But Stephenson could never have envisaged what he was starting when he suggested, in a centre-page feature in the *Daily Herald* of 22 June 1935, 'a Long Green Trail' from the Peak to the Cheviots which 'the feet of grateful pilgrims would, with the passing years, engrave on the face of the land'. The idea for the route was inspired by two American girls who asked Stephenson if Britain had anything similar to their country's 2,000 mile (3,200km) Appalachian Trail.

Although Stephenson campaigned patiently for years to open the Pennine Way, his hidden agenda was to clear up the long-standing access problems which still obstructed ramblers' rights to use the grouse moors of Kinder Scout and Bleaklow. When he began campaigning, only 180 miles (290km) of the route were on unopposed rights of way.

The Pennine Way was eventually declared open at a ceremony on Malham Moor on 24 April, 1965. The route passes many of the viewpoints we visit in this book. From the crag-rimmed plateau of Kinder Scout, with its fine view from Kinder Downfall, the route traverses Bleaklow and Black Hill to Blackstone Edge and Stoodley Pike. Into the verdant limestone country of Craven the route climbs past the

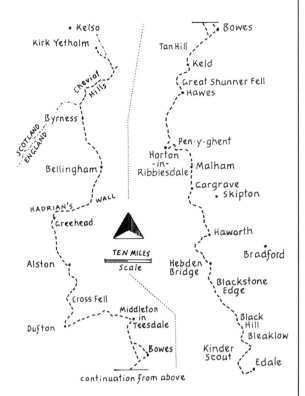

great amphitheatre of Malham Cove and over Pen-y-ghent, one of Yorkshire's famous Three Peaks. Passing Tan Hill, the highest pub in England, the route goes over 'Stainmoor's shapeless swell' between the Tees and Eden to the spectacular viewpoint of High Cup Nick and on to the highest point of the Pennines at wind-swept Cross Fell. From Alston, the Way strides north to Hadrian's Wall and Housesteads Fort, before plunging into the forestry belt of Northumberland to emerge triumphant at The Cheviot and the final descent to Kirk Yetholm.

Tom Stephenson would not have wanted a memorial of any kind, but the Pennine Way will remain his greatest achievement in a lifetime that was devoted to 'the right to roam'.

RIGHT _____

*The challenge of the Pennine Way. Walkers taking a north–south route on the famous footpath ascend the walled track by Harthwaite above Dufton towards High Cup Nick, with the slopes of Narrowgate Beacon rising ahead to the right*

ABOVE

*The spectacular view down the glaciated valley of High Cup Gill from High Cup Nick, as seen from the Pennine Way. The steep-sided valley sweeps down towards the valley of the River Eden in the middle distance, with the escarpment of Middletongue Crag prominent to the left and the Lake District hills beyond. Backstone Edge forms the skyline escarpment to the right, and Nichol Chair is among the dolerite crags on the edge of the combe to the right of the walker in the picture*

OPPOSITE

*The classic view of The Storr from across the blue waters of Loch Fada. The great basaltic cliffs of The Storr 719m (2,358ft) frown down on the bizarre, outlying leaning pinnacle of The Old Man of Storr which looks out across the low-lying island of Raasay in the Inner Sound, separating Skye from the mainland of Scotland*

But nothing prepares the walker for the first sight of the stupendous, crag-rimmed hollow of High Cup which falls away vertiginously at his feet. The breathtaking view is made even more impressive by the fact that it is so unexpected. Ahead the glacier-carved valley of High Cup Gill drops 305m (1,000ft) to the sweeping scree-lined pastures of the beck below, while the gentler green of the Vale of Eden spreads beyond to the blue hills of Lakeland in the furthest distance.

Standing up like a collar around the rim of the gorge, the hard volcanic rocks of the Whin Sill form upstanding columns of dolerite. The most famous of these columns is Nichol Chair, which is quite difficult to find in the crags to the right. This is said to be named after a Dufton shoemaker from the village in the valley below who not only climbed it, but proceeded to sole and heel a pair of boots on its miniscule summit. In truth, the story seems no more improbable than the actual achievement of the farmers who constructed the drystone wall which climbs almost vertically up Middle Tongue from the beck to the end of High Cup Scar to your left.

The Great Whin Sill is a prominent and

enduring feature of these northern hills. This volcanic intrusion of dolerite was laid down under water and baked the surrounding rocks into crystalline forms where vein metals like lead, silver and zinc formed. Because it withstands the forces of erosion better than the surrounding limestones, the Whin Sill forms prominent crags like those at High Cup, the waterfalls of High Force and Cauldron Snout in the valley of the Tees, the wall of rock on which Hadrian's Wall was constructed at Crag Lough and Cuddy's Crag, and the other ancient defensive sites of Bamburgh Castle and Lindisfarne. But the crowning glory of the Whin Sill is High Cup Nick, created by the powerful meltwaters of an Ice Age glacier some 10,000 to 15,000 years ago.

If you are not travelling north on the 250 mile (400km) Pennine Way, perhaps the best approach to the Nick is from the delightful village of Dufton in the Vale of Eden below. You approach the Nick on the Pennine Way (southbound) via Bow Hall Farm, south of conical Dufton Pike (another fine viewpoint, incidentally), ascending the northern rim past Hannah's Well on the Narrowgate Beacon path. Dufton is also a good starting point for the ascent of Cross Fell to the north, at 893m (2,930ft) the highest point of the Pennines. Because its summit is a broad stony plateau, however, the views are disappointing.

## BASALT:
### THE STORR AND THE QUIRAING, SKYE

There is nothing disappointing about the next pair of volcanic viewpoints, for which we have to go north of the Border and across the sea to the magical Isle of Skye. Norsemen are thought to have named this beautiful Inner Hebridean island from the words 'sky' and 'ey', meaning cloud island, and the jagged summits of the Cuillin and Trotternish are indeed highly productive cloud factories.

*Watching over his subjects and the lochan-jewelled, landslipped scenery of Skye's Trotternish peninsula, the 50m (165ft) pinnacle of the Old Man of Storr dominates the landscape north of Portree. This view of The Sanctuary is taken from the crumbling rocks of The Storr's 200m (650ft) eastern face, and looks beyond to the Sound of Raasay (left), Loch Leathan (behind the Old Man), and the distant saw-toothed ridge of the Cuillins*

But while the hard walkers and rock climbers will always be attracted to the firm gabbro and fine viewpoints of the Black Cuillin – the nearest thing we have in Britain to an Alpine landscape – the Trotternish peninsula at the northern tip of the island is in many ways a more fascinating landscape. The weirdly tilting basalt cliffs, towers and pinnacles of The Storr and The Quiraing are among the natural wonders of Britain, more reminiscent of the Myvatn area of that other Atlantic island which was also created by ice and fire, Iceland. Sixty million years ago, during the Tertiary period, the north of Skye was engulfed by wave after wave of red-hot lava which flowed from fissures deep in the earth's crust. Cooling quickly, the lava formed the fine-grained, quartz-dotted basalt which now covers the northern half of the island.

On the eastern side of the Trotternish peninsula, these massive sheets of basalt weighed down heavily on the underlying sandstones, causing them to collapse and creating some of the largest landslips in the British Isles – and some of its most spectacular scenery.

The cliffs of The Storr 719m (2,358ft), with its outlying pinnacle of The Old Man a prominent feature from the Portree road, is the highest point of the 15 mile (24km) Trotternish ridge, while the shattered cliffs of The Quiraing 543m (1,781ft), mark its northern climax.

The view of the leaning 50m (165ft) undercut tower of The Old Man of Storr from Loch Fada is one of the enduring images of Skye, and the walk up to the amphitheatre of The Sanctuary from the Loch Leathan car park is one of the most popular short walks on the island. The Sanctuary is an atmospheric place during those rare Skye spells of fine weather, but in mist it becomes an intimidating, even threatening, place where it is easy to believe that you are in the presence of the Norse gods who were thought to inhabit such places. You are surrounded by a chaotic array of weird pinnacles and fantastic buttresses which spring from the emerald sheep- and rabbit-cropped grass. One buttress is sharply pointed like a needle with two windows (or are they eyes?) punched through it, while another has the unmistakable profile of a Norse warrior, staring stonily out across Bearreraig Bay to Raasay and the mainland.

But lording over all his tottering subjects is The Old Man, an exclamation mark in basaltic lava, first climbed by the late Don Whillans in 1955. It was 'The Villain's' first unclimbed summit, a Very Severe route, the rock of which he later described as 'like coal, rotten and loose, you could prise chunks off without any bother at all'.

---

## ROUTES TO THE STORR AND THE QUIRAING

The isolated leaning pinnacle of The Old Man of Storr, towering above Loch Fada, is a prominent feature of the landslipped moorlands of Trotternish north of Portree on the Isle of Skye.

Park your car in the old quarry on the northern shore of Loch Leathan Reservoir. A path leads off north-west through the grass and heather to the strange collection of rocks known as The Sanctuary. Keep to the path which leads straight to the leaning and undercut pillar of the Old Man with the tapering Needle beyond. Make your way through the shattered boulder field to the base of the Storr cliffs in Coire Scamadal, with its tiny, jewel-like lochan. A careful climb through a break in the lower cliffs to the left will lead to a grand southern promenade along the crest of the buttresses and yawning gullies which form the basaltic Storr cliffs. The Old Man and his attendants can be glimpsed below, staring stonily out across the blue waters of the Sound of Raasay to the mainland peaks of Torridon beyond. After passing the summit cairn, 719m (2,358ft), follow the ridge as it bends down to the left around Coire Faoin. Eventually you will reach the moor and your car parked by the reservoir.

About 10 miles (16km) further north on the Trotternish peninsula lies the equally weird collection of basaltic rocks known as The Quiraing. This is usually reached by the fine high-level path which leads from the car park at Bealach Ollasgairte, the highest point on the Uig–Staffin road. The path leads beneath the crags of Maoladh Mor on an almost level route which leads directly into the heart of the strange rock garden known as The Quiraing, with the castellated rocky bastion of The Prison away to the right.

Alternatively, there is the somewhat boggier route up from the village of Staffin which climbs directly towards The Prison, which you pass to the left to reach the gloomy recesses behind The Needle and the secret prize of The Table, backed by the crumbling summit cliffs of Meall na Suireamach, 543m (1,781ft).

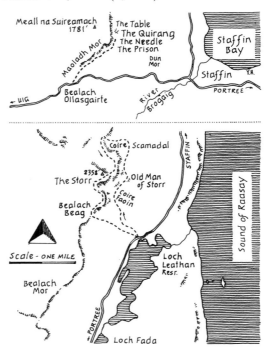

Walkers enjoy the wonderful view from the crumbling sandstone summit crags of Pen-y-Fan, the highest point in southern Britain. Across the green, bracken-covered shoulder of Twyn-y-Dyfnant to below and to the right, the view extends across the well-wooded valley of the Afon Tarell, with the patchwork hedged fields of the Usk Valley beyond that. We are looking directly towards the Brecon Beacons National Park's Mountain Centre near Libanus, on the Mynydd Illtyd Common

Fit and experienced walkers will want to ascend the forbidding 200m (650ft) summit cliffs of The Storr which back The Old Man for the fine views across The Sanctuary to the low-lying island of Raasay and south across the Storr lochs towards the saw-edged profile of the Cuillin. This is easily accomplished by traversing around the northern end of The Storr cliffs and above Coire Scamadal.

About 10 miles (16km) further north lies The Quiraing, another example of the astonishing powers of natural erosion. Looking up at the line of cliffs from the road just north of the tiny village of Staffin, you would hardly suspect what a wonderland is concealed behind their grim, grey bastions. Access to The Quiraing is usually from the highest point of the Staffin–Uig road at Bealach Ollasgairte, from where a fine, almost level, path takes the walker into the rocky heart of the mountain. Alternatively, you can traverse the boggy ground from Staffin and approach The Prison, the first forbidding outcrop of crumbling basalt, from beneath.

The green turf was alive with scampering rabbits on my first visit to The Prison, and we scrambled up through the labyrinth of rocky towers which seemed to brush the sky to emerge below the elegant tapering spire of the Quiraing Needle. It seemed to overhang the thin path which wound up and behind it into the heart of this awe-inspiring mountain wilderness. It's a stiff climb to reach the hidden secret of The Quiraing – The Table, a flat plateau of velvety grass that was once used to hide cattle away from the thieving eyes of raiders, and later as the spectacular setting for an annual shinty match.

Backed by the beetling cliffs of Meall na Suiramach, The Table offers stupendous views through the maze of pinnacles you have just negotiated, down to the crofts and golden sands of Staffin Bay, and across the blue Inner Sound to the isolated pre-Cambrian mountains of Applecross and Wester Ross, with Liathach, Beinn Eighe and An Teallach prominent.

As I rested on the grassy plateau of The Table on that first visit, I was startled by the sound of falling rocks from the cliffs behind. Turning quickly, I was surprised to see a sheep which had been grazing on the edge of the cliffs behind falling gracefully, as if in slow motion, clear of the rocks. It struck the ground in the litter of rocks at the foot of the cliff with a sickening thud, and bounced (it was in full fleece) until it finally came to rest near the foot of the path which led up to The Table. Unfortunately, the fall did not kill the sheep, although its back was obviously broken. It was our sad task to dispatch it to put it out of its misery.

## SANDSTONE: THE BRECON BEACONS

It's hard to underestimate the important part that erosion, by ice, snow, wind and rain, has played in shaping the British landscape, but in places like Skye and High Cup Nick you certainly get a good idea.

Another spectacular viewpoint, this time in South Wales, shows how ice and snow can actually build mountains out of rocks which were laid down in regular layers in a relatively settled period of geological time. The steep layered scarp slopes of the Brecon Beacons stand like a petrified tidal wave of Old Red Sandstone about to break over the green valley of the River Usk, south of Brecon. The distinctive peaks of Corn Du, Pen-y-Fan and Cribyn stand sentinel over the deep glacial cirques of Cwm Llwch, Cwm Sere and Cwm Oergwm, while the intervening ridges of Pen Milan, Cefn Cwm-llwch, Bryn-teg, Cefn Cyff and Cefn y-Bryn reach out like avaricious fingers clawing at the fertile plain of the Usk. The sedimentary sandstones and brownstones of the Beacons were laid down during the Devonian period some 400 million years ago, and later uplifted to a much greater height than their present altitude. But then came the great Ice Ages of the Pleistocene period which depressed and 'shaved-off' the top of the range, and left enormous glaciers in the lee of the hills, fed by the eternal ice and snows of the ice-caps above. Long after the Pleistocene glaciers had retreated, pockets of ice and snow were left on the north-facing slopes of the Beacons, resulting in the over-deepened cirques, or cwms as they are known in Wales, we see today. And the distinctive 'layer-cake' faces of sandstones and brownstones were sliced off by these frigid agents of ice and snow, later to be furrowed by rain and running water

# A ROUTE TO PEN-Y-FAN

Pen-y-Fan is not only the highest point of the Brecon Beacons, but it is the highest point in southern Britain, so the routes to its 886m (2,906ft) summit are understandably well worn and much frequented.

One of the most strenuous but rewarding routes is from the north, which entails a climb along the long rib of Bryn-teg from the hamlet of Bailea, just south of the village of Llanfrynach, near the county town of Brecon. The once-grassy but now badly eroded ridge is reached from a cart track, with the mural precipices of Pen-y-Fan to the right. The ever-steepening ridge finally reaches the summit of Cribyn, with one of the most famous, and most photographed, views of the flat-topped summit of Pen-y-Fan beckoning to the right. The grandeur of the north face of the reigning peak, seamed with gullies and ribbed with bands of rose-red sandstone and green grass, is now revealed in all its splendour.

Dropping down to the little col between the two peaks above Craig Cwm Sere, you gradually ascend to Pen-y-Fan and your objective, with Cwm Sere, source of the Afon Cynrig, below your feet. The view from the top includes the Black Mountains to the east, and to the west Fforest Fawr and Carmarthen Fan. Continue on to the flat table-top of Corn Du, if only for the bird's eye view of the circular Llyn Cwm-llwch, and the scene of little Tommy Jones' unfortunate demise.

Now you must retrace your steps to Pen-y-Fan and descend the grassy spur of Cefn Cwm-llwch to the ranges of Allt Ddu. Bear right across the fields to reach your point of departure.

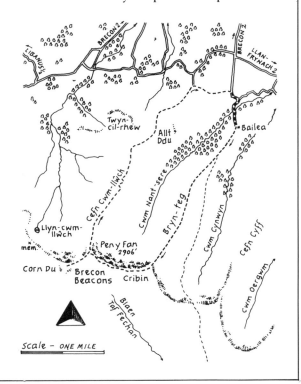

into the gullies and screes which scar the northern faces of hills like Pen-y-Fan.

It is a complicated story, and one which will not normally trouble the thousands who annually make the pilgrimage to the top of the reigning peak of Pen-y-Fan, at 886m (2,906ft) the highest point in southern Britain. But as John Constable said, we see nothing until we truly understand it, and it is interesting to see how such grand mountain forms can be built by the agents of destruction, as well as by those of creation. The Brecon Beacons have long acted as an escape for the industrial communities of South Wales, and they continue to provide an irresistible magnet to school parties and trainee Royal Marine com- mandos from the nearby camp at Sennybridge. But they should never be underestimated, as the sad story of little Tommy Jones illustrates.

Five-year-old Tommy was the son of a miner from Maerdy at the head of the Rhondda Valley. In August 1900 he had been taken by his father to visit his grandparents who lived in the last farm up the deep valley of Cwm-llwch. Walking up from the station in Brecon, the pair parted at the now ruined farm of The Login when Tommy's cousin, 13 year old Willie John, ran down to meet them. The two lads set off alone back the quarter of a mile to Cwm-llwch, but darkness was falling, and Tommy began to cry and started back to his father who was coming up behind. What

*The 'layer-cake' northern face of Pen-y-Fan, at 886m (2,906ft) the reigning summit of the Brecon Beacons, is well seen in this view from the steep north-east ridge of Y Cribyn, across Cwm Sere. The walkers in the picture are approaching the summit on the loose, shaley sandstones which make up most of the Beacons. Peeping over the shoulder of Pen-y-Fan to the right of the walkers, in the centre of the picture, is the third of the Beacons, Corn Du*

happened next is a mystery, for little Tommy never reached his father, nor the farm. Searches were set up and rewards were offered, but all to no avail. It was to be twenty-nine days before his body was found, 686m (2,250ft) up on the ridge above Llyn Cwm-llwch and 2 miles (3km) above the farm he was heading for. The spot where Tommy Jones was found is marked today by a simple obelisk, a monument to those who might underestimate these beguiling Beacons.

Erosion is a serious problem on some of the routes to these handsome summits, notably on the Bryn-teg, Cribyn, Pen-y-Fan and Cefn Cwm-llwch horseshoe. A pleasant variant, which saves the splendid view across the valley of the Usk towards the unknown hills of central Wales until the last, is to approach from the easier southern slopes from the Pontsticill Reservoir and Taf Fechan forest walks, past the Neuadd Reservoirs. Alternatively, there is the shorter but very popular and badly eroded variant from the Storey Arms on the A470 Brecon–Merthyr Tydfil road.

## SYMOND'S YAT

Just across Offa's Dyke lies another spectacular geomorphological viewpoint which shows the landscape-creating power of another apparently gentle agent – the River Wye. The view from Symond's Yat is justly famous and regularly features as a subject on those 'Beautiful Britain' calendars. The sweeping curve of the river through the well-wooded gorge is lovely at any time of the year, but perhaps especially so in autumn when the dying year tints the trees in a million subtle hues.

The Wye, then known as the Afon Gwy, rises high on the slopes of Pumlumon, one of those secret central Welsh hills seen from the Brecon Beacons. Passing through Builth Wells, Hay-on-Wye, Hereford and Ross-on-Wye, it does the job of Offa's Dyke for much of the latter part of its journey to the Severn, acting as the boundary between England and Wales. At Symond's Yat it breaks through the limestone outlier of the ancient Forest of Dean in what geologists call an incised meander. About two million years ago during the Pleistocene period, the Wye probably flowed in a gentle meander over a flat plain. The sea level then was about 180m (600ft) higher than it is today, but as the sea level dropped and the land was uplifted, the Wye's speed and cutting power increased dramatically, producing the spectacular gorge of Symond's Yat.

RIGHT

*A peregrine's eye view of Symond's Yat from Yat Rock, in the Forest of Dean, Gloucestershire, as autumn colours start to steal in among the rich woodlands which cloak the banks of the River Wye. This view is looking northwards as the Wye enters its great sweeping horseshoe bend around Huntsham Hill, in the left distance. The bracken-covered hill on the right is Coppet Hill, beyond which lies Goodrich and its famous red sandstone castle. The peninsula on which the Yat Rock stands is protected by the ancient earthworks of an Iron Age hillfort*

# MASTERS OF THE AIR

The elegant peregrine falcon has been described as 'the perfect flying machine', but it is only one of the masters of the air that you are likely to encounter as you labour up to that longed-for viewpoint. Many of our most beautiful and exciting birds of prey make their homes in the uplands, where there is still a measure of protection from persecution. They include the swashbuckling and moustachioed peregrine, and there is nothing quite so thrilling as the sight of a peregrine 'stooping' at up to 200mph (320kmph) on its prey.

In the remoter Scottish glens, and increasingly further afield, you may be lucky enough to spot the king of the birds, the majestic golden eagle. With its 2m (6ft) wingspan, an eagle, once seen, is never forgotten.

Often confused with the golden eagle but actually much smaller is the buzzard, a broad-winged raptor which is often seen effortlessly riding the thermals above the hills. This is our most common large bird of prey and its mewing cry is for many the essence of the uplands.

The well-wooded hillsides of Central Wales now harbour the last stronghold of the fork-tailed red kite, once a common scavenger over the streets of London, but now extremely rare.

The dashing merlin is a blackbird-sized falcon which pursues its prey across the moors in a hectic, twisting-and-turning chase, while the common kestrel, or windhover, is as likely to be seen these days riding the wind over a motorway as nesting on a hillside crag.

Ground-nesting like the merlin is the hen harrier, a long-legged raptor which is now very rarely seen on our moors.

The prey of these masters of the upland air includes the plump red grouse and the ptarmi-

*The merlin is the smallest European falcon, and sadly, the only British bird of prey whose numbers are currently in decline.* (Dennis Green/RSPB)

gan in Scotland, both of which are managed for commercial shooting.

Other ground-nesting birds in the hills include waders like the curlew with its haunting, bubbling call; the rarer golden plover, 'the guardian of the moors'; the twite and the dunlin.

LEFT
*A riverside view up towards the crags of Yat Rock, on the skyline (top left) from Coldwell Rocks on the opposite bank of the winding River Wye in the Forest of Dean. We are looking downstream as the Wye bends around Huntsham Hill. Yat Rock occupies the narrowest point of the oxbow, and one day in distant geological time, the river is destined to break through, leaving the flat meadows of The Stalls isolated*

**DORSET COAST, WHITE NOTHE** _____
*Looking west on the Dorset Coast Path from below the
great chalk headland of White Nothe – the highest point
on the Dorset Coast – where peregrine falcons once bred.
On the horizon in the distance across Weymouth Bay,
the long, low shape of the Isle of Portland can be seen,
like a huge surfacing whale. The landslipped cliffs below
White Nothe (the name means White Nose) now form
part of a nature reserve famous for its butterflies and
birdlife*

The best approach to the popular viewpoint of Symond's Yat is from the convenient car park across the road, but for a pleasant longer walk, use the Forestry Commission's forest trail and descend to the river, crossing by the ferry to explore the Lord's Wood peninsula and the caves named after King Arthur and the Seven Sisters, and returning by the riverside path with its superb views.

The most famous residents of the Symond's Yat gorge today get even better views than the thousands of human visitors. Peregrine falcons returned to one of their traditional breeding sites on the Yat Rock in 1982 after an absence of about thirty years. Since then, the Royal Society for the Protection of Birds has instituted a special peregrine watch with telescopes and special displays at the most popular viewpoint so that visitors can enjoy and appreciate the sight of these magnificent raptors.

I was privileged to be let into the secret of the Symond's Yat peregrines long before the decision was taken to 'go public', and if the RSPB's action encourages greater protection of these masters of the air, the experiment will have achieved its laudable objective. The peregrines are now as much a part of the Symond's Yat scene as its famous view, and they give it a *frisson* of excitement which was not there before.

## CHALK: THE DORSET COAST

For spectacular views of a former breeding site of peregrine falcons, where they might hopefully return one day, we must travel to the South Coast of England. Brian Jackman's official guidebook to this part of the Dorset Coast Path promises 'a crash course in geology', and it is no exaggeration. The section between Osmington Mills and Lulworth rollercoasts for 5 miles (8km) over dazzling chalk cliffs and springy downland turf which, in my experience, is unmatched in England.

The walk starts at the pretty chocolate-box village of Osmington, a confection of thatched grey-stone cottages and flower-filled gardens. Strike off across the fields to the hamlet of Osmington Mills on the coast where you join the waymarked coast path behind the thirteenth-century Smugglers Inn. Climbing steadily to the ugly concrete eyesores of the World War II pillboxes on top of Bran Point, you reach the first 'summit' of the walk. The view west from here is superb, with the low blue bulk of the Isle of Portland, source of some of the finest building limestone in Britain, seeming to float like a basking whale on the sparkling waters of Weymouth Bay. Weymouth itself shows as a necklace of glittering windows, strung together by the breakwaters of Portland Harbour.

Descending from Bran Point, you enter a low-lying wooded section of the coast path, after crossing a series of stiles and footbridges. These wooded valleys are known locally as 'gwyles' and this one eventually emerges at the seaside bungalows of the hamlet of Ringstead, known in Thomas Hardy's novels as Ringsworth Shore.

Just inland is the deserted medieval village of Ringstead, a victim either of the Black Death or of raiding French pirates, depending on which story you prefer to believe. Across gently sloping downland now, the path climbs above the chalk and shale landslips of Burning Cliff, which gets its name from an outbreak of spontaneous combustion which took place there in the 1820s.

The next objective is the great chalk headland of White Nothe (or Nose), with the 47ha (115 acre) Whitenothe Undercliff nature reserve nestling in the landslips beneath. White Nothe is the highest point on the path, where the dashing peregrine falcons once bred on the precipitous cliffs below the undistinguished coastguard cottages which now occupy the summit. The views from here are spectacular, back across Weymouth Bay in the direction you have come and eastwards towards our objective of Lulworth Cove.

RIGHT

*The famous natural arch of Durdle Door, one of the showplaces in British geology, on the Dorset coast, west of Lulworth Cove. It was formed by the sea eating away the relatively softer chalk and leaving behind the soaring flying buttress of harder Portland stone which is Durdle Door. In the chalk cliff of Bat's Head, just to the west, a wave-carved 'mousehole' marks the start of what will eventually become another natural arch like this one*

The descent from White Nothe is steep and can be tricky, but you will soon reach the col between Bat's Head and Swyre Head and a suitable lunch stop. Below, the translucent sea works tirelessly at the 'mousehole' in the foot of Bat's Head, beyond the biscuit-coloured beach.

But the highlight of the walk beckons and you must walk on up and over Swyre Head towards the flying buttress of Durdle Door, where the soaring natural arch has been carved out of solid Portland stone by the sea which has worn away the softer surrounding strata.

The last climb is to Hambury Tout from where Lulworth Cove can be seen, besieged by a massive car park and its associated hordes of holiday-makers, but still impressive in its natural architecture. Here, if you are really lucky as you make the steep climb up the slopes of Bindon Hill above the perfect scallop-shell of the cove, you might just spot, as I did, the insignificant toffee-brown butterfly which takes its name from the site. The Lulworth Skipper was not discovered until 1832 and is still confined only to this part of the Dorset coast. It is to be hoped that, like the peregrine, the skipper can extend its range to add further wildlife interest to this classic geological location.

FACTBOX

| | GR | MAP |
|---|---|---|
| Beacon Hill, Leicestershire | SK511148 | LR129 Nottingham & Loughborough |
| Brimham Rocks, North Yorkshire | SE212650 | LR99 Northallerton & Ripon |
| Farleton Fell, Cumbria | SD545805 | LR97 Kendal & Morecambe |
| High Cup Nick, Cumbria | NY745262 | OL31 Teesdale |
| The Storr, Skye | NG495541 | LR23 North Skye |
| The Quiraing, Skye | NG454693 | LR23 North Skye |
| Pen-y-Fan, Brecon Beacons | SO012217 | OL11 Brecon Beacons – Central |
| Symond's Yat, Hereford & Worcester | SO563160 | OL14 Wye Valley & Forest of Dean |
| White Nothe, Dorset | SY772809 | LR194 Dorchester & Weymouth |

LEFT

*The great banded chalk cliffs of White Nothe rise 167m (548ft) above the crashing breakers of the English Channel on the Dorset Coast long distance path. This view looks westwards towards the peninsula of the Isle of Portland which breaks the horizon across the blue waters of Weymouth Bay*

# 2
# FOLKLORE
# AND LEGEND

Long, long ago, in the dreamtime before human history, the British Isles were inhabited by a race of extraordinary beings called giants who roamed the land, warring and quarrelling with one another and using their superhuman strength to create landmarks and whole landscapes in their wake. Wherever you go in Britain there are place-names or folk-tales which recall this mythical race. From the weird pinnacle of The Old Man of Storr on the Isle of Skye to the low chalk Gogmagog Hills of East Anglia, and from St Michael's Mount in Cornwall to the ghostly Grey Man of Ben Macdhui in the lonely Cairngorms, almost every striking natural feature seems to have a giant story associated with it.

Are these stories merely fairy-tales, invented to frighten the children? Or do they provide evidence of a dimly recalled folk memory which was used to explain the apparently inexplicable? Some authorities believe that giants were a Celtic creation, used by the bards to explain the monuments left by their prehistoric forebears. It is not surprising that the storytellers attributed the mysterious structures in the landscape, such as Stonehenge and the other stone circles, rows and megaliths, to the work of these gigantic super-humans, for these impressive monuments seemed to be beyond the primitive technology of their day. They therefore concluded that these ancient landmarks were the work of the super-natural, or even of the Devil himself. And when credibility was finally stretched to breaking point, giants seem to have been replaced by legendary folk heroes, some of whom, like Cornwall's Jack-the-Giant-Killer or East Anglia's Tom Hickathrift were poor boys who overcame the local giant and stole both his power and his treasure.

Folklorists suggest that the advent of the folk hero, most of whom had distinctly saintly qualities, represents the triumph of Christianity over pagan superstition. Indeed, some folk heroes were saints, like St George who is said to have overcome the dragon on Dragon Hill below the Uffington White Horse, with its splendid views across the eponymous vale in Berkshire.

Uffington, with its strange, stylised White Horse carved in the hillside, is one of several candidates for the site of the Battle of Mount Badon, where King Arthur, one of the most long-lived and popular of Britain's folk heroes, is said to have fought his decisive action against the invading pagan hordes of Saxons. Others include Liddington Castle, also on the prehistoric Ridge-way above Swindon, or Badbury Rings in Dorset, both of which are also the sites of Iron Age hillforts (see Chapter 3). The generally accepted opinion is that Arthur was the leader of a guerrilla army of free-ranging cavalry troops who were victorious in a series of battles against the Saxons in the troubled days which followed the Roman withdrawal from Britain in the early fifth century.

The Hollywood image of King Arthur and the Knights of the Round Table wining and dining in chivalrous splendour at Camelot is a medieval invention which owes little to fact. Life in fifth-century Britain was much more likely to be hard, short and brutal, and the image of gallant knights in shining armour, as well as being an obvious anachronism, seems to have sprung from the fertile imagination of poets like Thomas Malory. His *Le Morte D'Arthur*, published in 1485, was in any case most probably a reaction against the contemporary internecine strife of the Wars of the Roses, and the name Camelot was the invention of a French romancer writing seven centuries after King Arthur's lifetime. But Arthur, 'the Once and Future King', remains a remarkably persistent talisman, ready and waiting still at various sites throughout Britain to come back to save the country when it is in direst peril. What is interesting about heroes like King Arthur is the similarity of the legends associated with them in various parts of Britain. The story that Arthur and his knights are sleeping in a cave waiting for their moment of recall is found from Cadbury Castle in Somerset, the favoured site for Camelot, to Sewingshields Crag on Hadrian's Wall, both of which sites we will visit later. Arthur obviously enjoyed a good view too, as his Seat, overlooking Edinburgh, illustrates.

Equally ubiquitous is Robin Hood, the happy-go-lucky outlaw who roamed Sherwood Forest robbing the rich to give to the poor. In many ways, Robin Hood fulfils exactly the same role as King Arthur – the local hero who fought against the injustices of the wicked invading oppressor – although in Robin's case it was the Norman overlords who had to be overcome, and he is usually depicted as a dispossessed Saxon. There are one or two clues that Robin Hood may actually have existed as an outlaw in the royal hunting forests of Sherwood or Barnsdale in the north Midlands, perhaps in the thirteenth or fourteenth centuries. Edward II, concerned about the depredation of robbers in his forests, is known to have travelled north in 1323. But equally, Robin is said to have been a supporter of Simon de Montfort, who was outlawed after the Battle of

## GIANT HILLS

According to Geoffrey of Monmouth's *History of the Kings of Britain*, written in the twelfth century, the British Isles were originally 'uninhabited except for a few giants' who were particularly populous in the Westcountry. They were eventually vanquished by the descendants of the defeated Trojans of classical Greece, led by Brutus, and the last to be killed was Gogmagog (see Chapter 3).

But belief in giants and child-eating ogres had always harked back to a distant and heroic past, and many apparently inexplicable natural and man-made features in the landscape have been attributed to these superhuman beings. As late as the sixteenth century, the people of Dundee were said to have destroyed a tribe of man-eating ogres who lived in the hills above the Tay, and fossil mammoth bones discovered near Plymouth in the last century were firmly believed by the local population to be those of Gogmagog. Some people who live near the uninhibited Cerne Abbas Giant still believe him to be a representation of a slaughtered Danish giant.

We walk to several 'giant hills' in this book, from the buried giants of the Wrekin and Wandlebury, near Cambridge, to the wise old Welsh giant, Idris, who sits for ever on his seat overlooking the Mawddach estuary. But there are many other giant hills throughout Britain, especially in their traditional stronghold of the 'Wild West'. St Michael's Mount in Cornwall is said to have been built as a stronghold by the local giant Cormoran who quarried the massive granite boulders which form the island from the nearby hills, before he dumped them in the sea. Other giant features in the Cornish landscape include the Giant's Cradle on Trecobben Hill, where the giants supposedly dragged their victims before murdering them; the Giant's Pulpit at Carn Boscawen; and the Giant's Chair, on the rocky coastline 3 miles (5km) south-east of Land's End.

Giants were not confined to the Westcountry, however, and another mythical giant, Wade, is attributed with building the Roman Road which is still known as Wade's Causeway across the North York Moors, as well as building the castles at Pickering and Mulgrave. A giant who lived in a cave on the Malvern Hills once saw his wife talking to a man on the village green of Colwall and threw a huge stone down on top of her. Legend often credits giants with the building of hillforts, and long barrows and other tumuli are referred to as 'giants' graves' throughout Britain. Isolated boulders or standing stones were similarly often thought to be the work of giants who had been competing with one another or the Devil in gargantuan hurling matches.

Evesham in 1265 and was a supporter of Thomas of Lancaster's rebellion in 1322. The oldest surviving ballad, 'The Lytell Geste of Robyn Hode and his Meiny' (band) dates only from the fifteenth century. The truth is that Robin Hood, like King Arthur, is an immortal and universal hero, blessed with superhuman powers and always ready to come to the aid of those in distress. There are strong arguments to suggest that he may even be a reincarnation of the Celtic Green Man, a pagan god of the forests who was created from the needs and discontents of the medieval peasantry. Many of Robin's named landmarks are certainly in remote and secluded places and are found much further afield than his traditional stamping grounds.

Many of the landmarks associated with giants or fairies, King Arthur or Robin Hood, also provide spectacular viewpoints, as if these ancient super-heroes and villains needed to watch over the ordinary mortals who lived in their shadow. In this chapter we will explore some of the viewpoints and the stories, both fact and fiction, which are associated with the landscapes that have perpetuated the names of these mythical figures for so many generations.

## The Wrekin

Some hills seem to have a presence and a relationship with their neighbourhood which is as often psychological as it is physical. Examples include Coniston and its Old Man, Horton in Ribblesdale and Pen-y-ghent, and Glastonbury and the surrounding Somerset Levels and Glastonbury Tor. They often had folk-tales associated with them and stories linked to imminent changes in the weather, usually related to the amount of cloud cover on the hill in question. Such hills 'drew the thunder' and created their own weather, according to local people.

One such hill is the Wrekin, symbol of home for Salopians and still the subject of a local toast: 'All friends around the Wrekin.' The 'forest-fleeced' Wrekin, as A. E. Housman called it, (see p. 179) is not the highest hill in Shropshire, but because it rises so suddenly from the plain it seems to command more attention than many

greater heights in this lovely county. Local author H. W. Timperley admitted that to Shropshire people, the Wrekin was as much a spirit as a hill, and 'when you go to it, the underlying mood or feeling is that of a pilgrimage'. Few hills have a greater 'spirit of place' than the Wrekin and, as might be expected, it has attracted its share of legends. The most popular story of its origin concerns a malevolent Welsh giant who had a grudge against the people of the county town of Shrewsbury. He set off with a great load of earth to dam the River Severn and so flood the town and drown its citizens. On his way, he met a cobbler who was carrying a sackful of boots and shoes for repair, and he asked him for directions to Shrewsbury. The cobbler, realising the giant's evil intention, claimed that, having just walked from Shrewsbury, he had worn out his entire load of boots and shoes. The giant groaned in despair and dumped his load of earth where he stood, thus creating the Wrekin.

Another story tells of two warring giants who built the Wrekin from earth which they had dug from the bed of the Severn. One day they quarrelled, and one threw his spade at the other, creating the narrow cleft in the hill called the Needle's Eye. Then a raven pecked at one of the first giant's eyes, causing him to shed the tears which now form the Raven's Bowl, a small pool on top of the rock called the Bladder Stone. Finally, the second giant slew the first and buried him under Ercall Hill to the north of the Wrekin, where, it is said, he can still be heard groaning at the dead of night.

Many walkers and climbers speed west along the M54 around the new town of Telford, intent on reaching the greater heights of Snowdonia and

RIGHT

*On the roof of the Midlands on The Wrekin. This view from the pre-Cambrian rocks of the summit crags looks south-east towards the Severn Gorge, with the four cooling towers and chimney of the power station at Buildwas prominent in the distance. Just downstream from there, the Industrial Revolution was born in the iron furnaces of Coalbrookdale, and the world's first iron bridge gave its name to a site now famous in the world of industrial archaeology. The lake surrounded by trees in the centre distance is known as Devil's Dingle*

# A Route to The Wrekin

Park in one of the former quarries in Ercall Lane and walk north towards the motorway bridge across the M54. Turn right alongside the motorway fence across a footbridge and a lane before turning south near the hamlet of Steer-away to enter the cool shade of Limekiln Wood. Paths lead through the mixed woodland where there are tantalising glimpses of the wooded slopes of the Wrekin to the right. You emerge at The Hatch where you must cross the minor lane which runs between Huntington and Cluddley. Keeping to the right-hand edge of another tongue of woodland, you emerge onto another lane which links Cluddley and Little Wenlock. By now the other Shropshire hills – the Long Mynd, Caer Caradoc and Wenlock Edge – are in sight. Turn right, descending the lane for about 230m (250yd) to a stile on the left which gives access to a path which leads into the woods that clothe the eastern slopes of The Wrekin itself.

The broad track leads up through the trees to meet eventually the main ridge track at Little Hill, the southernmost end of the range. You are in open country now and the views open up on all sides as you tramp up the broad track which is formed of ancient pre-Cambrian rocks. About 90m (100yd) before the summit toposcope and OS trig point is the prominent rocky outcrop known as the Needle's Eye. The well-trodden track leads gradually down to the northern end of the hill. Passing a radio mast, go through Heaven Gate and Hell Gate, which mark the entrances to the Iron Age hillfort of the Cornovii. Dropping down off the hill, you descend through the trees again past a white cottage to reach Ercall Lane. Follow this back to your car past the Lawrence Hill Reservoir on your left. Ercall Hill is on your right, where, according to the legend, a defeated giant lies buried beneath the trees.

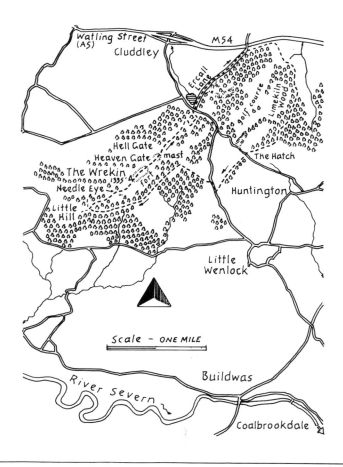

completely ignoring the shaggy wooded slopes of the Wrekin immediately to the south. They are missing one of the finest viewpoints in the country which extends, it is claimed, across seventeen counties. If you climb no other hill in Shropshire, you should climb the Wrekin. The last time I made the pilgrimage to its bald 407m (1,335ft) summit was on a scorchingly hot summer's day, when I met a man on the summit from Moseley, in Birmingham, who said that to climb the Wrekin was his 'weekly escape'. I could certainly understand that, for from where we sat we could admire a stunning panoramic view which took in the blue outline of the Malvern Hills 40 miles (64km) to the south; the neighbouring Shropshire hills of the Clees, wooded Wenlock Edge and the Long Mynd fronted by the shark's tooth of Caer Caradoc; and the misty shapes of the Berwyns, the first hills of Wales, 30 miles (48km) to the west.

There are several routes to the toposcope which marks the summit of the Wrekin, most of which pass through the beautiful mixed woodlands which fringe the summit of ancient pre-Cambrian rocks. The steepest approach is via the Needle's Eye from the direction of Eaton

*Brooding like a shark's fin above the green-hedged Shropshire landscape, the Wrekin is a conspicuous landmark for miles around. Small wonder then that it occupies such a prominent place in Salopians' affections and in their folklore. This view of the Wrekin and the Shropshire Plain is from just below Robin Hood's Butts, at the northern end of the Long Mynd range – the highest ground in the county*

Constantine, but the easiest way is to walk from the road which runs between the Wrekin and the Ercall. Or you can climb up through the cathedral-like beeches from the straight minor road of the Wrekin Course to the north. Approaching from the north or east, you emerge on the shoulder of the hill on a broad track which passes through the rocky clefts of Hell and Heaven's Gate, marking the entrance of the Iron Age hillfort that rings the summit. The ancient tribesmen of the Cornovii who built the fort certainly had a bird's eye view of the Roman invaders as they constructed their imperial highway of Watling Street across the lowlands below, but there is no legend of a final battle here, like that of Caractacus's legendary stand on neighbouring Caer Caradoc.

*The view southwards over the black silhouette of Cranberry Rock (foreground) from the Stiperstones. The green folds of Linley Hill are in the middle distance and beyond them, the valley of the West Onny river and the border town of Bishop's Castle. Clun Forest and the first hills of Wales are on the distant horizon*

OPPOSITE

*The sinister Devil's Chair crowns the bristling rocky ridge of The Stiperstones. Rising like the spines of a dinosaur from the heather-covered moor, the quartzite tors were once the scene of extensive lead mining, and many shafts still exist beneath the surface. There are many legends associated with the Stiperstones, and they impart a threatening, evil atmosphere to the place, even on a still summer's day when the delicious bilberries are in fruit*

## THE STIPERSTONES

Shropshire and its wild, western 'border country' hills like the Wrekin seem to spawn larger-than-life legends. Another hill which has a special place in Shropshire folklore is the spiny ridge of the Stiperstones, hidden by the bulk of the Long Mynd in our view from the Wrekin. The Stiperstones attract myths and legends as easily as the clouds and storms which so often rage about them. The highest point, at 528m (1,731ft) is known as The Devil's Chair, and when mist covers the shattered quartzite rocks of the summit, local people still claim that 'the Devil's on his throne'.

One of the tales associated with the Stiperstones is similar to that attached to the Wrekin — the Devil is said to have dropped an apronful of stones on the summit which he intended to use to fill up Hell Gutter, a ravine on the slopes of the hill. Another story is that the Devil hates England above all countries, and when the Stiperstones sink down to the plain, England will perish. So when the clouds are down on Stiperstones summit, the Devil is said to be sitting on his chair

## DEVIL HILLS

Just as giants, King Arthur and Robin Hood were used by superstitious country people to explain away ancient or natural features in the landscape, so too was Old Nick, or the Devil, given his place in the folklore of the countryside. Some folklorists believe that, with the advent of Christianity, Satan took the place of the Norse God Odin, or Woden, as the Wild Huntsman of the Skies. It was he who chased his pack of baying hounds across the skies on wild winter nights, striking terror into the hearts of all who saw him, for to see the hunt could result either in your being carried off to a distant land, or, worse still, certain death. It is a legend still spoken of in the wild hill country of Dartmoor.

The Devil is frequently associated with the dropping of stones, such as those on the Stiperstones in Shropshire and the Devil's Nightcap or Agglestone near Studland on the Dorset coast, or with stone circles where dancers on the Sabbath were turned to stone by a piper who was, in fact, the Devil, such as the stone circles at Standton Drew in Somerset and the Rollright Stones on a Cotswold ridge in Oxfordshire.

Many hills with good views are named after the Devil – for example, the fine viewpoint of the beech-topped Iron Age hillfort of Chanctonbury Ring on the South Downs of Sussex. An eerie place at the best of times, it has acquired an even more sinister appearance since the storm in October 1987 decimated the stately trees. The story is that the Devil will appear if you run seven times backwards around the clump of trees at midnight on Midsummer Eve. When he appears he will offer you a bowl of porridge in exchange for your soul or the granting of your greatest wish. The nearby Devil's Dyke, which slices spectacularly through the rolling downs south of Poynings, was supposedly an attempt by Old Nick to dig through to the sea and drown the local populace which had recently accepted Christianity. The similarly known Devil's Dyke near Newmarket in Suffolk is thought to be a defensive rampart constructed in the seventh century against the invading Mercians.

The Devil's Punchbowl is a popular viewpoint on the heathy sandstone ridge near the Surrey village of Hindhead and the scene of the brutal murder of a sailor in 1786. The murderers were hanged and gibbeted near the spot. North of the border, 5 miles (8km) north-west of Moffat in the heart of Scott's Border Country, the Devil's Beef Tub is a gloomy natural hollow once used for hiding stolen cattle. The Devil's Chimney on Leckhampton Hill, near Cheltenham (see also p. 136), is a wonderful viewpoint across the green acres of the Severn Valley from the western escarpment of the Cotswolds. It is also an example of how strong the belief in Old Nick still is, for the 15m (50ft) high limestone pinnacle was left by local quarrymen who believed that it rose straight from Hell.

in the hope that his weight will sink the hill and bring about the destruction of the nation.

The Stiperstones also feature prominently in *The Golden Arrow*, the first and one of the best-known novels of Mary Webb who lived in the village of Pontesbury at the northern end of the ridge. She called the range Diafol (or Devil's) Mountain, and wrote: 'It drew the thunder, people said. Storms broke suddenly round it out of a clear sky. No one cared to cross the range near it after dark . . . It remained inviolable, taciturn, evil.'

A friend of mine put one of the best-known legends of the Stiperstones to the test by timing his walk to the strange wild summit so that he reached it exactly at midnight on the longest night of the year for a promised rendezvous with the Devil. It was the ancient festival of Samain, the beginning of the Celtic year when the barriers between man and the supernatural are lowered, and locally it was believed that it was the night when all the witches and ghosts in Shropshire gathered to elect their king. But my friend failed to raise Old Nick as he sat on his chair at the appointed time. All he saw was a disturbed lapwing 'circling the moon like a witch on a broomstick'. Perhaps that's just what it was.

The Stiperstones are easily reached from the minor road between Bridges and Pennerley, where there is a parking place near the col between the main hill and Nipstone Rock. You make your way over the heather and bilberries between the strange scattered outcrops of quartzite, which date from the Ordovician period, and through a landscape which is more reminiscent of Dartmoor or the Scottish Highlands than Shropshire. There is surface evidence of lead mining here, and another legend tells of Wild Edric, a Saxon leader who was said to be imprisoned below the Stiperstones for submitting to William the Conqueror, and whose knocking could be heard underground by the miners.

The view from the Stiperstones ridge on a clear day is magnificent, with the isolated height of Corndon Hill in the immediate foreground to the west, and Offa's Dyke and the Welsh hills behind. Looking south, Linley Hill and conical Black Rhadley Hill stand out, while to the east, the huge whaleback of the Long Mynd broods menacingly.

## CADER IDRIS

Not quite visible from here, but mentioned by Mary Webb in the first paragraph of *The Golden Arrow* as part of the view from John Arden's cottage at Pontesbury, the long escarpment of Cader Idris is home to another legend concerning a giant. Cader Idris, at 892m (2,927ft) is perhaps

---

## A ROUTE TO CADER IDRIS

Perhaps the finest route of the many which lead to the summit of Cader Idris is that which starts from the lovely lake and valley of Tal-y-llyn. From the lakeside, pass through the Idris Gates, which were erected by the soft drinks company which used the name of the mountain for its product, and walk through the encroaching rhododendrons before crossing a footbridge and a stile to reach open country. This well-used path climbs steeply through the trees which flank the rocky bluff of Ystrad-gwyn, with the stream which issues from Llyn Cau making merry music to your right. The path leaves the trees and rises through bracken-covered slopes to the outflow of Llyn Cau.

The late Walter Poucher described this viewpoint as 'one of the wildest places in all Wales' and the whole of Craig y Cau, with the Pencoed Pillar prominent to the left, is revealed in front of you, reflected in the still waters of the llyn. The Craig y Cau cwm is part of a national nature reserve, so please 'take nothing but photographs, and leave nothing but footprints'. Our route skirts the shore of the llyn to the right to ascend the steep slopes of Craig Lwyd and eventually to reach the summit of Craig y Cau.

From here, the route to the reigning peak of Pen y Gadair descend to the col and then along the east-west ridge to the large summit cairn. An interesting diversion can be made to the northern summit of Cyfrwy, along the rim of the cwm which encloses the tiny eye of Llyn y Gadair at its feet.

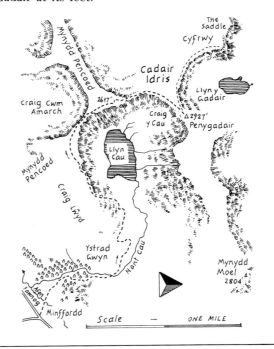

*The view westwards along the rocky ridge from the slopes of Mynydd Moel towards Pen-y-Gadair, the 892m (2,927ft) summit of Cader Idris, with the tiny tarn of Llyn-y-Gadair beneath. To the left of the summit is Craig Cau, and the route up from Tal-y-Llyn. To the right, the summits of Cyfrwy and Carnedd Lwyd stretch on into the distance above the Mawddach Estuary*

*Looking down into the Chair of Idris from the summit of Pen-y-Gadair. Nestling in the bottom of Cwm-y-Gadair is the jewel-like lake of Llyn-y-Gadair, sheltered by the jagged Cyfrwy arête, with its prominent Table about halfway up. Beyond that, the pastoral green fields and woods of the Mawddach Estuary run down to Barmouth and the Irish Sea, which can just be seen on the extreme left of the picture*

the most English of Snowdonia's mountains and a great favourite with walkers and climbers from the West Midlands. Yet it takes its name from a Welsh giant, Idris Gawr, who used the summit as his chair. The name means the chair of Idris, which is usually supposed to be the glacial hollow which encloses Llyn-y-Gadair, cradled at the foot of the summit precipice of Pen-y-Gadair. According to the legend, Idris was a giant of many parts – poet, philosopher and astronomer – who studied the stars from his rocky observatory on the summit.

A real Idris existed, however, who was a prince of Merioneth during the seventh century, and it is just as likely that the mountain was named after him. He is mentioned in ancient Welsh documents as Idris ap Gwyddno, a hero who died defending his country at 'the Slaughter of the Severn' – a battle against Irish invaders.

The other great legend attached to the mountain is shared with Maen du'r Arddu on Snowdon. It is that whoever falls asleep on the summit will awake either as a poet or a madman. I have climbed Cader in all weathers and although I

have never fallen asleep on the summit, I have often thought that I was mad to be there. And there is certainly a kind of poetry in the ascent of Cader from the south, through the estate of the soft drink company which used the name of the giant for its product.

Leaving the lovely lake of Tal-y-llyn, you pass through the famous Idris Gates and over a footbridge before climbing around the rocky bluff of Ystrad-gwyn and up into the impressive glacial cirque of Cwm-y-Cau. Reflected in the still waters are the grim green precipices of Craig Cau towering ahead. Our route skirts the left-hand side of the crystal tarn and climbs right to gain the summit of Craig Cau, with superb views down the cwm towards Tal-y-llyn. The reigning top of Pen-y-Gadair is now obvious ahead, and you are soon there.

The view from the summit is one of the finest in Wales, with the glistening golden sands of the Mawddach Estuary crossed by the taut black thread of the Barmouth bridge commanding most immediate attention. Beyond that, looking north beyond the intervening heights of the Harlech Dome, it seems that the whole of Snowdonia, to the black triangle of Yr Wyddfa, is laid out before you. Looking south over the precipitous Craig Cau, the elephantine lump of Pumlumon Fawr fills the skyline 20 miles (32km) away.

## The Afanc of Glaslyn

Many of the Welsh llyns and the Scottish lochs, notably Loch Ness and Loch Morar, have tales of monsters lurking beneath their cold waters. Less well known, perhaps, is the fabled Afanc said to inhabit the dark blue waters of Glaslyn, the highest lake on Snowdon's eastern flank. The story goes that this fearsome monster lived in a deep pool in the River Conway near Betws-y-Coed, now sometimes known as the Beaver Pool. From here it periodically emerged to cause dis-astrous floods, ruin crops and drown cattle. But the Afanc had one weakness – beautiful young maidens – and that was how the local people decided to trap it. A courageous young girl was persuaded to act as the decoy to tempt the Afanc from the pool and as soon as it emerged, the local populace set on it and bound it up in strong

chains. Using teams of oxen they dragged the furious monster across country up the Lledr Valley past Dolwyddelan and over the shoulder of Moel Siabod to the head of the Gwynant Valley. Up into the depths of Cwm Dyli by Llyn Llydaw they hauled the protesting monster until they reached the remote enclosed lake of Glaslyn, then known as Llyn Ffynnon Las, or the Lake of the Blue Fountain. Releasing the chains, they dropped the Afanc into the dark blue depths where it has lived ever since. I wonder how many walkers tackling the final climb of the Zig-Zags on Snowdon's popular Miners' Track have looked down into the still waters of Glaslyn and seen those mysterious ripples, which could not have been caused by the wind . . .

## The Fairy Princess of Llyn-y-Fan-fach

The legend of Llyn-y-Fan-fach, a hidden lake cradled by the huge sweeping precipices of Bannau Sir Gaer, which with Bannau Brycheiniog forms the highest points of the Black Mountain west of the Brecon Beacons, is equally long lived. It concerns a young farmer's boy from the village of Myddfai in the valley to the north who grazed his father's cattle in the upland pastures around the remote lake in the heart of the mountains. One day, he was amazed to see a beautiful girl emerge from the lake and proceed to comb her lovely long hair by the shore. He immediately fell in love with this vision of loveliness and vowed to marry the fairy princess. She tempted him by refusing the offer of newly baked bread on the first two occasions, but finally agreed to wedlock. However, she warned the farmer that if he struck her on three occasions after they were married, she would return to the lake. The princess's dowry included as many fairy sheep, cattle, goats and horses as she could count in a single breath; all of which magically emerged from the lake, just as she had done. The marriage was a happy one and the couple had three fine sons. One day, the farmer tapped his wife in jest on the shoulder, and she tearfully reminded him of her warning that he should not strike her. Two years later, he patted her again, this time to comfort her because she was crying. That was the second blow. The

*An early morning view of the scree-buttressed sandstone cliffs of Bannau Sir Gaer and the northern scarp of the Black Mountain south-west across Waun Sychlwch from Fan Foel, the northernmost spur of the range. Llyn-y-Fan-fach lies cradled in the glacial hollow beneath the mural red cliffs of Bannau Sir Gaer with Bwa'r Llyn enclosing the lake to the south in the far distance*

third happened when the fairy princess was laughing at a funeral and the farmer touched her lightly on the arm to stop her. The fairy returned to their farm on the hillside above Myddfai, then she led all the cattle, sheep and goats back up the mountain to Llyn-y-Fan-fach, where they all disappeared under the black waters, leaving the desolate farmer alone on the shore. The princess did not forget her sons, however, and she returned to see them one day as they mourned her by the lakeside. She gave Rhiwallon, the eldest, a leather bag which she said contained the healing secrets of the Other World, and she showed them all the healing herbs which grew on the mountain and how to use them to cure human ailments. So the Physicians of Myddfai were created, and the three brothers became the most famous healers in Wales and were appointed to the court of the Prince of South Wales. Generation after generation of the family inherited the gift of healing and the last known

descendant was still practising medicine in the late nineteenth century.

The easiest approach to Llyn-y-Fan-fach is from Llanddeusant village where there is a youth hostel for overnight accommodation. The route up the valley of the Afon Sawdde via the hamlet of Blaenau, although now mainly on water company roads and tracks, probably follows the route taken by the young Myddfai farmer when he first took his animals up to the lake. When you emerge at the lake it is disappointing to see that it is now enlarged and used as a reservoir, but even the sight of the dam wall and pump-house cannot detract from the grandeur of the surroundings. The mural sandstone precipices of Bannau Sir Gaer form an imposing backdrop and lead up to the reigning eastern-facing summit of Bannau Brycheiniog, 802m (2,631ft), which can be reached easily by climbing up the slopes of Tyle Gwyn to the right and following the path which leads around the lip of this impressive escarpment, now the property of the Brecon Beacons National Park authority.

## King Arthur's Last Stand: Bwlch-y-Saethau

A few miles to the west, just outside the county town of Carmarthen, is a small hill known as Bryn Myrddin, or Merlin's Hill, where King Arthur's faithful adviser and magician is said to be entombed in a cave. In a Welsh version of the Arthurian legend *Llfyr Du Caerfyrddin*, or *The Black Book of Carmarthen*, after Arthur's demise, Merlin wandered the land in misery for fifty years before

Overleaf

*The view east from just below the summit of Snowdon across Glaslyn, in shadow below, to the larger Llyn Llydaw beyond. The Miners' Track by the shores of the lakes, and the Pyg Track higher up the slopes, can be seen winding their way towards the summit. The sharply pointed peak in the centre of the picture is Crib Goch, whose serrated ridge is the ultimate challenge for the Snowdonia scrambler and represents the most exciting route to Snowdon's summit. In the distance to the right are the sunlit sepia slopes of Moel Siabod with the barren Glyders to the left*

# ROUTES TO SNOWDON

Snowdon summit was once described by the Prince of Wales as 'the highest slum in Britain', and it certainly suffers more than most from a seemingly never-ending invasion of trippers. The rack-and-pinion mountain railway, opened in 1896, transports thousands annually who cannot, or will not, walk to the summit hotel, the café and the tremendous view. But the finest way to appreciate Snowdon's tarnished grandeur is still to walk, and there are seven main routes to the top, following the main ridges. One of the most popular is the Miners' Track from Pen-y-pass at the summit of the Llanberis Pass. This easy but heavily restored track follows the route taken by the miners who worked the copper mines on Snowdon's eastern flank. It follows the causeway across Llyn Llydaw before it reaches the steep and now overtly engineered track of the Zig-Zags below Bwlch Glas.

The Pyg Track also starts from Pen-y-pass, but rises more directly to Bwlch Moch – the Pass of the Pigs – after which the route was probably named. It passes on a fairly level but high route under the crags of Crib Goch before joining the Miners' Track at the Zig-Zags. The Crib Goch route, part of the classic Snowdon Horseshoe, sticks to the crest of that serrated and exposed ridge, and is for experienced scramblers only. Of the western approaches, the Snowdon Ranger track starts from the youth hostel of the same name on the A487, and zig-zags over easy ground to reach the crest of the great black precipice of Clogwyn du'r Arddu and the railway and Llanberis track at Bwlch Glas.

The Beddgelert, or Rhydd-ddu, path starts from the former South Snowdon station and rises steeply to the broad shoulder of Llechog before swinging east to the saddle of Bwlch Main, a spectacular viewpoint itself, and the summit.

The Watkin Path, named after Sir Edward Watkin, was opened in 1892 to commemorate a visit by W. E. Gladstone. It starts from Nant Gwynant to the south of the massif, past the ruins of Plas Cwm-llan, and then bears right to climb steadily to Bwlch-y-Saethau, scene of King Arthur's last battle with Modred, between Yr Wyddfa and Lliwedd.

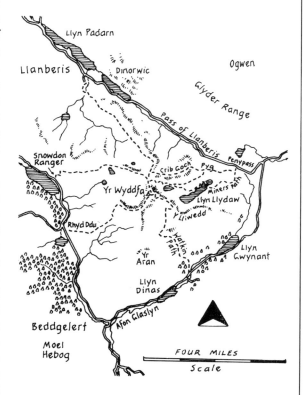

The last route from Llanberis is the longest, safest but least interesting, and climbs steadily parallel to the railway before passing above and to the left of Clogwyn du'r Arddu and reaching the summit via Bwlch Glas. At Clogwyn Station, there is a spectacular bird's eye view down into the jaws of the Llanberis Pass.

*Looking east over the fairy lake of Llyn-y-Fan-fach from Bwa'r Llyn, the nick in the north-west summit of the Bannau Sir Gaer escarpment on the Black Mountain of Carmarthen. The dark prow of the reigning peak of Bannau Sir Gaer breaks the skyline, with the northern spur of Bannau Brycheiniog and Fan Foel behind. Afon Sawdde winds down from the lake to the left*

becoming a prophet and teaching his spells to a woman called Vivien. His punishment for passing on his secrets was eternal entombment under the hill. This happened after the last fateful battle between Arthur and his traitorous nephew Modred, which one legend states was fought on the long rocky col between Yr Wyddfa, Snowdon's summit, and the neighbouring peak of Lliwedd. The col is still known as Bwlch-y-Saethau, the Pass of the Arrows, because some say that Arthur, like the later king, Harold, died in a hail of arrows in the battle. Others claim that Arthur, and Modred who had treacherously sided with the Saxons, fought themselves to a standstill on the col overlooking the Afanc-haunted Glaslyn and eventually, both died from their wounds. The faithful Sir Bedivere carried the broken body of his king down to the waters of Llyn Llydaw, where Arthur was borne away in a black barge by three beautiful women. Bedivere gathered the remainder of the Knights of the Round Table and took them back up the steep rock slopes of Lliwedd to a cave where they still wait for his second coming.

Cynics will claim that the legend is no more than a fairy story or yet another Arthurian myth dreamed up by imaginative Celtic bards. After all, Arthur's last stand has been sited in various places, and there are similar stories of his sleeping knights on the Eildon Hills in Scotland (see Chapter 5), on Sewingshields Crag, Northumberland, near Richmond Castle in Yorkshire and on Craig-y-Dinas in Glamorgan, among many others. But that does not explain the frightening experience of a young shepherd boy in the early nineteenth century who climbed onto the precipitous east face of Lliwedd to recover a stray sheep. He found himself opposite the mouth of a deep cave and, being curious by nature, he looked inside. There leaning against the dripping walls of the cave were the serried ranks of King Arthur's knights. Astonished, he turned to flee but banged his head on a bell which was hanging from the roof. The knights awoke with a shout and the shepherd boy retreated in blind panic down the crag, eventually losing his reason as he tried to explain the unbelievable story to his friends.

Bwlch-y-Saethau, which was formerly marked by a great cairn known as Carnedd Arthur, is part of the famous Snowdon Horseshoe, the classic one-day excursion of the massif. Having made the steep ascent of Crib Goch and negotiated the airy pinnacles of its serrated ridge, the walker gains the 1,085m (3,560ft) summit of Yr Wyddfa, with its stupendous view which will be described in Chapter 5. You then make the steep descent with its spectacular bird's eye views of Llyn Llydaw to the broad stony col where Arthur met his death.

Ahead from Bwlch-y-Saethau is the noble prospect of the jagged West Peak of Lliwedd, one of the most dramatic scenes on the entire Horseshoe, and a well-worn path leads to its summit. To the left, the popular Watkin Path winds up from the verdant valley of Nant Gwynant, with its string of glacial lakes 600m (2,000ft) below.

Of all the many proposed sites for King Arthur's last battle, this surely is the most appropriate, in the heart of this great mountain fastness which in Welsh is named Eryri – the abode of eagles.

*The great hooded cowl of Lliwedd, Snowdon's south-eastern peak, frowns down over the legendary scene of King Arthur's last stand on the col of Bwlch-y-Saethau, in the bottom right-hand corner of the picture. Lliwedd's black shadow reaches out towards the blue waters of Llyn Llydaw, with the shapely peak of Moel Siabod in the distance. The famous Snowdon Horseshoe walk descends from Snowdon's summit to Bwlch-y-Saethau and over the jagged crest of Lliwedd, to descend to the eastern limit of Llyn Llydaw and down to Pen-y-Pass*

## CADBURY AND
## GLASTONBURY TOR

Just as there are many proposed sites for King Arthur's last stand, there are several candidates for his legendary stronghold of 'many tower'd Camelot'. The one most favoured by the scant archaeological evidence is the wood-ringed Iron Age hillfort of South Cadbury, near Yeovil in Somerset, chiefly because it is one of the few which has been systematically excavated. Cadbury Castle, as it is known locally, has been identified with King Arthur's castle at least since the fifteenth century, and it is in the heart of the Arthurian Westcountry, within sight of Glastonbury Tor – the Avalon of legend. King Arthur and his knights are said to lie sleeping in the heart of

*The view from the south-east ramparts of Cadbury Castle, looking south towards isolated Parrock Hill 179m (587ft), with the gorse-clad beacon of Corston Hill beyond. The Yeo Levels stretch away to the right towards Yeovil and Thomas Hardy's Wessex*

Cadbury's hill, and Queen Camel, a village near its foot, is believed to be another possible site of the Battle of Camlann where Arthur died in mortal conflict with Modred.

But what gives Cadbury precedence over all the other possible Camelots are the excavations conducted by Professor Leslie Alcock which proved conclusively that the site was occupied by an important sixth-century warrior chieftain who reinforced the old Iron Age defences with ramparts of stone and timber. In the interior of the defences, a post-built aisled hall of the same period was discovered, and a plentiful scatter of pottery indicated a fairly extensive and important settlement. We will probably never know if this powerful British leader really was King Arthur of the legends, but as you walk around the 8ha (18 acre) hillfort of South Cadbury, its defensive ditches still obvious on the ground, and look across the broad green Somerset Levels to the tower-topped Tor of Glastonbury, it is easy to believe that he was.

We follow that line of sight to the fabled Isle of

Avalon and Glastonbury Tor for our next viewpoint, and on the way dispel some of the myths which have been associated with this stunning landmark. Undeniably, there is a sense of magic about the Tor which rises so abruptly from the surrounding flood plain, but some of the nonsense which has been written about the site, including a 'zodiac' of astrological signs inscribed in the features of the landscape, irrespective of the date of those features, is astonishing. Using the same dubious principles, a leading landscape historian recently 'discovered' images of Mickey Mouse, Goofy and Winnie-the-Pooh in the same landscape! Glastonbury is also said to be the hub of the 'ley' system which links multi-age sites across the country in a network of lines of 'unseen power'.

Traditionally, Glastonbury is the last resting place of King Arthur, and his grave was said to have been uncovered in the grounds of the abbey in the twelfth century. A lead cross, which disappeared in the seventeenth century, was found on the grave, inscribed with the words: 'Here in the Isle of Avalon the famous King Arthur lies buried.' (continued on p. 78)

*The dedication to St Michael of the fourteenth-century church which once topped Glastonbury Tor is significant. St Michael, the serpent-slaying soldier of God, was often used by the Church to 'christianise' previously pagan hilltop sites. A look at the number of hilltop churches which are dedicated to St Michael will show how widespread was the practice. All that is left of St Michael's church today is the tower; the rest of the cruciform building was destroyed in an earthquake and never rebuilt*

*Was this King Arthur's 'many tower'd Camelot'? Tree-ringed Cadbury Castle, seen here from the neighbouring height of Corston Hill Beacon, is the archaeologists' favourite. The embankments of the Iron Age hillfort, reinforced by an important sixth-century warrior chieftain who just could have been King Arthur, can plainly be seen crowning the summit which towers above the prosperous farmlands of Somerset. Whitcombe Farm, on the right, marks the site of a deserted medieval village*

ARTHUR'S SEAT

*The remains of the Arthur's Seat volcano, as seen from another of Edinburgh's seven hills, Calton Hill, close to the city centre. Flat-topped Arthur's Seat 251m (823ft) is seen in the centre, with the steep, sill-formed cliffs of Salisbury Crags forming an escarpment to the right. The Royal Palace of Holyroodhouse is on the left in the mid-distance below Arthur's Seat, with the Firth of Forth and Musselburgh in the far distance to the left*

With its Christian connections with Joseph of Arimathea and the famous Christmas-flowering thorn tree, Glastonbury has been long established as a place of pilgrimage and the modern astro-archaeologists are merely perpetuating an ancient tradition. When I am travelling west, I cannot pass by the mysterious magnetic shape of the Tor without climbing up to the ruined fourteenth-century tower of St Michael's Church, if only to admire the stupendous 360-degree view of the rhine-crossed, willow-dotted levels which may, or may not, have been the last resting place of King Arthur.

## ARTHUR'S SEAT

Exactly the same kind of magnetism tempted me to climb Arthur's Seat, the 251m (823ft) plug of an extinct volcano which gives such a commanding view over Edinburgh, when I first visited the Scottish capital many years ago. The Arthur's Seat volcano originally towered 1,000m (3,280ft) above sub-tropical lagoons in the Carboniferous period, but today it lies peacefully within the royal park of Holyrood House. The view from its red-basalt-crowned summit extends over the entire city – 'the Athens of the North' – to the blue line of the

## EDINBURGH'S HILLS

Edinburgh, the spiritual capital of Scotland, has been called 'the Athens of the North', and it shares a feature with another classical capital, for, like Rome, it is founded upon seven hills. A native son, Robert Louis Stevenson, described it as a 'precipitous city', but added 'Edinburgh pays cruelly for her high seat in one of the vilest climates under heaven'. But he was writing in the days when Edinburgh was also known as 'Auld Reekie' when smoke pollution undoubtedly added to that 'vile' climate.

There is no better way to appreciate Edinburgh's fine architecture, closes and parks than to climb up to one of its seven hills, such as Arthur's Seat with its panoramic views across the city to the distant Pentland Hills and the Firth of Forth, described in this chapter. Stevenson noted that Calton Hill was the best place from which to view Edinburgh Castle and Arthur's Seat, both of which are the 'plugs' of extinct volcanoes. The views along Prince's Street and of the Old Town, the heart of the capital, are truly magnificent, and collectors of follies and monuments will be richly rewarded, for it was Calton Hill which earned Edinburgh that comparison with Athens. The unfinished National Monument was supposedly a copy of the Parthenon and a grand memorial to the Scots who died in the Napoleonic Wars, but

funds ran out in 1822 after only twelve columns had been erected.

The circular neo-classical monument to the philosopher Dugald Stewart which overlooks Prince's Street was built by William Playfair also in 1822, while the Gothic Nelson's Monument by Robert Burn (1807) is supposed to represent an upturned telescope. The Old and New Observatories, both of classical design, complete Calton Hill's eccentric array of architecture.

Castle Hill is perhaps the most commanding viewpoint in the city and may originally have been the site of an Iron Age hillfort, so it can truly be called Edinburgh's cockpit and birth-place.

Corstorphine Hill to the west is the site of Edinburgh Zoo and it offers a wide panorama of the city, with Arthur's Seat prominent. The Clemiston Tower here was built to celebrate the centenary of Sir Walter Scott's birth in 1871. Basaltic Craiglockhart Hill overlooks the pretty village of Swanston and the south-west corner of the city, while the nearby Braid Hills give fine views to Ben Lomond to the north-west and the Pentland Hills to the south. A little closer to the city is Blackford Hill, home of the present Royal Observatory, set in its own park which overlooks the sylvan green southern suburbs of the city.

Ochils beyond the Firth of Forth in the north, and the rolling summits of the Pentlands to the south. Landmarks in the city beneath include the castle on its rock (formed by a vent from the Arthur's Seat volcano), the Scott Monument and Waverley Station in Prince's Street, and the colonnades of the unfinished National Monument on Calton Hill. Arthur's Seat apparently gained its name during the fifteenth-century revival of interest in Arthurian romances, inspired by Malory.

*A misty day in 'Auld Reekie'. This view north-west from just below the summit of Arthur's Seat shows Edinburgh Castle prominent in the centre of the picture. It crowns the summit of its volcanic plug, which is thought to have been an outlying vent of the massive Arthur's Seat volcano, active during the Carboniferous period about 350 million years ago. The 73m (240ft) spire of Tolbooth St John's on Castlehill in the Royal Mile – the highest spire in the city – is prominent to the right of the castle*

# A Route to Robin Hood's Stride

The author on the rocky ridge which separates the twin towers of Robin Hood's Stride. The ground around Robin Hood's Stride – which is also known locally as Mock Beggar's Hall – is a rich hunting ground for the antiquarian, with a stone circle and the remains of a sizeable Romano-British settlement.

The route starts from the workaday White Peak village of Elton. Take the footpath through All Saints churchyard which leads across the stone-walled fields into Dudwood Lane. Turn left and go down the hill. At the bottom of the hill go straight ahead up through a stile onto a track which eventually runs into the ancient Portway – a route used since prehistoric times and paved in places. This leads unerringly onto Harthill Moor where the outcrops of Robin Hood's Stride and Cratcliff Tor are revealed.

The Portway passes between these two strange gritstone features in a largely limestone landscape. Allow plenty of time to explore both

of these fascinating and mysterious places. In the fields to the north can be seen the four large standing stones which are all that remain of the Nine Stones Circle, dating from the Bronze Age.

Rejoining the Portway, go left through gates and stiles to reach Cliff Lane, opposite the entrance to Harthill Moor Farm. Turn right, following the Limestone Way signs, and start the descent towards Alport. Turn left off the lane at a gate which leads into a conifer plantation. This pleasant path leads around Castle Ring Hill, the site of yet another Iron Age hillfort, and crosses a small stream.

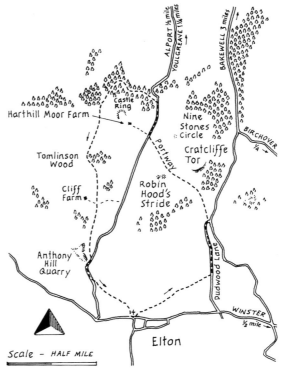

Scale – HALF MILE

You now head due south on a well way-marked path, around Tomlinson Wood and across the track to Cliff Farm, to descend back into Elton past Anthony Hill Quarry on your right. Just as you reach the road, note the line of stone water-troughs which were once used by horses working at the quarry.

## ROBIN HOOD'S STRIDE

But what of that other great folk-hero, Robin Hood? My choice of viewpoint to celebrate the great outlaw may seem surprising, for it is not in Sherwood, nor even in Nottinghamshire. North Derbyshire, in fact, can lay as good a claim to be the haunt of the man in Lincoln green as anywhere else in Britain. If placename evidence counts for anything, the moors surrounding the valley of the Derwent seem to have been a stronghold of Robin Hood's Merry Men, and the grave of his faithful lieutenant, Little John (or John Little, to use his real name), is there for all to see between two stunted yews in his native churchyard of Hathersage. Above the village, on the popular rock-climbing gritstone outcrop of Stanage Edge, is Robin Hood's Cave, a favourite bivouac for generations of climbers, and the pub beneath Birchen's Edge, another favoured rock-climbing spot, is also named after the outlaw.

We will seek Robin Hood further south, on the minor road between Alport and Grangemill, where a weird gritstone tor has long carried the name of Robin Hood's Stride. Two fluted pinnacles of gritstone top the tor about 9m (30ft) apart, proving that Robin Hood had supernatural powers if that was the length of his stride. The pinnacles are known to climbers as the Inaccessible and Weasel Pinnacles, and they gave rise to the other local name for the tor, Mock Beggar's Hall. Silhouetted in the fading light of the setting sun, the strangely isolated outcrop can look just like the chimneys of a ruined building.

The view from the saddle between the two pinnacles is one of the finest in the White Peak, for Robin Hood's Stride is a gritstone outcrop almost entirely surrounded by limestone. It extends east towards the equally strange outcrops of Rowtor Rocks, over Birchover, with the Bronze Age necropolis of Stanton Moor, topped by its radio mast, to the left. Looking south, the hillside village of Winster can be seen beneath Wyns Tor, while to the east and north, almost the whole of the stone-walled White Peak plateau, cut through by the hidden dales of Bradford and Lathkill, is revealed, with the village of Youlgreave prominent.

Due north, the great wooded gash of the Wye Valley can be seen, backed by the sepia Eastern Moors above Chatsworth. Beyond that, in the blue distance, the dim outline of the northern moors of the Dark Peak form the horizon.

The area around Robin Hood's Stride has long been sacred. In the meadows immediately north of the outcrop can be seen the four great monoliths of the Harthill Moor stone circle which dates from the Bronze Age, and traces of a Romano-British settlement have also been found in the surrounding area. The cobbled track which leads up to the Stride from the road is the prehistoric Portway, one of several ancient trackways which cross the Peak, and under the frowning gritstone escarpment of Cratcliff Tor immediately opposite lived another fugitive from society. Hidden behind an enormous spreading yew tree at the foot of the tor is the Hermit's Cave, where a medieval holy man (could it have been Friar Tuck?) lived in quiet seclusion. Now railed off, the cave has a vigorous carving of the crucifixion in the rock of the back wall, presumably executed by the hermit himself. It is a secret, magical place where the wind stirring through the needles of the ancient protective yew seems to whisper of its sacred past.

## THE WITCHES OF PENDLE

Further north in the Pennines, the brooding presence of another dominating hill has spawned a further crop of legends, but with a more sinister background based on historical fact. Such is the powerful influence Pendle Hill exerts over the Ribble and Burnley valleys in south Lancashire that it was once thought to be one of the highest hills in England. According to an old couplet: 'Ingleborough, Pendle and Pen-y-ghent are the highest hills twixt Tyne and Trent.' We now know, of course, that the 'Big End' of Pendle only reaches 557m (1,832ft), but such is its domination of the surrounding valleys that it is not surprising that local people held it in greater esteem. Pendle is another 'storm-gatherer' hill, and another local rhyme forecasts:

> When Pendle wears a woolly cap
> The farmers all may take a nap.
> When Pendle Hill doth wear a hood
> Be sure the day will not be good.

ABOVE

ABOVE

The gritstone tor of the Inaccessible Pinnacle at Robin Hood's Stride in the Peak District towers above the purple flowers of rosebay willow herb in this picture taken at the height of summer. The Inaccessible Pinnacle is the western tower of the two which make up Robin Hood's Stride – but generations of rock climbers have regularly disproved this epithet. The deeply fluted tower a few yards to the east in this weird outcrop is known as the Weasel Pinnacle

RIGHT

The inspiring view from just beneath the summit of Pendle Hill, in the heart of Lancashire witch country. The author admires the patchwork walled and hedged landscape of the ancient Forest of Pendle southwards towards the pretty village of Barley, with the blue waters of the Ogden Reservoir backed by the dark conifers of Fell Wood on the right. It was here that the founder of the Quaker movement, George Fox 'was moved to sounde ye day of ye Lorde' in 1652, and where access pioneer Tom Stephenson first fell in love with the hills

But Pendle is perhaps best known for the stories of seventeenth-century witchcraft which were popularised in Harrison Ainsworth's melodramatic novels. The tales of Mother Demdike, Old Chattox and Alice Nutter were all based on fact, for the Forest of Pendle was rife with witchcraft and black magic in the early 1600s. Three generations of witches were said to operate in the area, led by Old Mother Demdike who lived at Malkin Tower in the shadow of Pendle, near the pretty village of Newchurch-in-Pendle. This 80 year old hag, a half-blind beggar, cheated the hangman by dying while she was imprisoned in Lancaster Castle Gaol, but nine other prisoners, all from the Pendle district, were sent to the gallows in 1612. They had been charged with desecrating graves, communing with imps and the Devil, plotting to blow up Lancaster Castle, and committing at least sixteen murders. How the wealthy and well-educated gentlewoman Alice Nutter, who lived at nearby Roughlee Hall, became involved with the miscreants is one of the many mysteries of the Pendle witches.

But not all the stories associated with Pendle Hill are as sinister as this. Forty years later, when George Fox was 'moved of ye Lorde to goe atoppe of it', he experienced the revelation which was the inspiration for his Society of Friends and the beginning of the Quaker movement. 'I was moved to sounde ye day of ye Lorde & ye Lorde lett mee see a top of ye hill In what places hee had a great people', he wrote later.

Pendle also inspired a 13 year old textile millboy, who first climbed the hill in wooden clogs from his home in Whalley at the end of his first week at work in 1906. The view that met Tom Stephenson on that crisp February morning was to change his life, for he dedicated himself to a lifetime of fighting for the rights of others to roam freely on the mountains and moors. 'It was breathtaking,' he recalled to me seventy years later. 'I saw range after range of snow-capped hills – Ingleborough, Pen-y-ghent – all of which I didn't know then, but which were to become old friends. Oh gosh, I just hadn't realised that this whole new world was on my doorstep. I made up my mind that day that this was for me.' Millions of visitors to our national parks and users of the Pennine Way should be eternally grateful for Pendle Hill and the effect it had on the late Tom Stephenson.

The best approach to Pendle's inspirational summit is to follow Tom's footsteps, up from the car parks among the upturned slabs of the Nick o' Pendle between Padiham and Clitheroe. It is a steady, easy climb on a broad track over Apronful Hill and Black Hill before you follow the deep valley of Ogden Clough to the final black peat hags and groughs of Barley Moor, on the long final pull to the bare summit.

The shorter tourist route up Pendle approaches from the pretty village of Barley to the east. Every Hallowe'en, it becomes a winding river of light as up to two thousand torch-carrying walkers aim to reach the witch-haunted summit by midnight, presumably hoping to meet Old Mother Demdike.

The view from the summit on a clear day explodes at your feet, revealing a glorious patchwork of fields, farms and woods extending down over the nucleated village of Barley directly beneath. The glistening plantation-fringed waters of the Black Moss and Ogden Reservoirs sparkle to the south, backed by the long whaleback of Boulsworth.

The last time that I was on Pendle was with my partner in this book, photographer John Cleare, who has travelled all over the world on major mountaineering expeditions. As we sat in the lee of the summit, absorbing the superb view and being buzzed by swooping swallows and swifts as they snapped up insects from the summer air, John turned to me and said: 'Y'know, there's nowhere in the world quite as beautiful as England.' I readily agreed.

LEFT _____

*The long ridge of Pendle Hill rising to 557m (1,832ft) as seen from Padiham Heights near Black Hill Wood, across the valley of the Sabden Brook. Just above the forestry plantation on the extreme left of Pendle Hill is Deerstones Quarry, where a giant's footprints are said to be embedded in the rock. The legend is that this is where he landed after striding off Hameldon Hill seven miles to the south. His next short step took him to Apronful Hill on Pendle's west flank, from where he aimed a huge boulder at Clitheroe Castle in the valley below*

FACTBOX

| | GR | MAP |
|---|---|---|
| The Wrekin, Shropshire | SJ629082 | LR127 Stafford & Telford |
| Stiperstones, Shropshire | SO364984 | LR137 Ludlow & Wenlock Edge |
| Cader Idris, Gwynedd | SH711131 | OL23 Snowdonia – Cader Idris |
| Glaslyn, Snowdon | SH617546 | OL17 Snowdonia – Snowdon |
| Bannau Brycheiniog, Brecon Beacons | SN825218 | OL12 Brecon Beacons – West |
| Bwlch-y-Saethau, Snowdon | SH614542 | OL17 Snowdonia – Snowdon |
| Cadbury Castle, Somerset | ST628252 | LR183 Yeovil & Frome |
| Glastonbury Tor, Somerset | ST512385 | LR183 Yeovil & Frome |
| Arthur's Seat, Edinburgh | NT275730 | LR66 Edinburgh & Midlothian |
| Robin Hood's Stride, Derbyshire | SK224623 | OL24 White Peak |
| Pendle Hill, Lancashire | SD805415 | LR103 Blackburn & Burnley |

# 3

# MONARCHS OF ALL THEY SURVEYED

A glance at Sheet 137 of the Ordnance Survey's 1:50,000 Landranger map, covering Ludlow, Wenlock Edge and the surrounding area of Shropshire, unfolds many stories for the assiduous map-reader. We are in the very heart of the Welsh Marches here, and, as might be expected in this troubled borderland, there are many examples of defensive structures visible in the landscape. Ludlow's great red sandstone keep, built by Roger Montgomery, Earl of Shrewsbury, in the eleventh century to repel Welsh raiders, succeeded the many smaller mottes and baileys, such as those scattered along Offa's Dyke, with a

*These ancient beeches fringing the hillfort of Chancton-bury Ring high on the South Downs in Sussex were depleted in the October 1987 storm. More than half were felled in the unexpected hurricane. The hillfort is protected by a single bank and ditch enclosing 0.3ha (³/₄ acre), with a single entrance on the western side. It is one of the few hillforts in Britain which also contain the later remains of a Roman temple, and there was a legend that you could raise the ghost of Julius Caesar and his army by counting the (uncountable) trees*

classic example at New Radnor on the edge of the map. This landscape was shaped by the need to defend, a landscape of conflict and war. Later, the fortified manors of Stokesay Castle, Bromfield, and Richard's Castle tell of more settled times, and the manors of Wilderhope (see Chapter 5) and Croft Castle resemble the stately homes found in the more peaceful areas of Britain.

But perhaps the most striking feature of the map for the landscape historian is the number of forts, camps and earthworks marked in the Gothic typeface which the OS uses, rather imprecisely, to indicate a 'non-Roman' antiquity.

blanket Forestry Commission plantations, but many others command the same sweeping views over the countryside which first attracted their builders over two thousand years ago.

It therefore goes without saying that the modern rambler exploring the countryside for good views could do worse than to follow the example of his Iron Age predecessors and to search out these ancient sites for their outstanding panoramas, as we aim to do in this chapter.

The Ordnance Survey's map of Iron Age Britain, which only records the large hillforts (as these structures are generically known), shows about three thousand of them, concentrated mainly in the south and west of Britain. Radiocarbon dating has shown that most of the hillforts of Britain were built between 700 and 500BC, though many were modified on a number of occasions, right up to the Roman invasion in the first century AD. Recent research has shown that some may have been originally constructed as early as the Bronze Age and some may even have had their antecedents in the defended sites of the late neolithic period. Archaeological excavations have shown that hillforts could have been built and occupied for a thousand years or more, so they have been more or less permanent features of the landscape, culture and folklore of Britain for many generations.

The question which has still not been resolved satisfactorily is, what was the purpose of these structures? They were certainly important enough to employ a huge amount of manpower and organisational skill in their construction. A typical medium-sized, 9ha (22 acre) fort could have taken as much as 175,000 man hours, or 100 men 220 days, to build.

The name 'hillfort' can give a misleadingly military connotation to what was their main use, although there is no doubt that, if only by virtue of their situations, most must have been primarily defensive. But the idea that they were all the last outposts of the 'Ancient Britons' who fled there, Asterix-style, in the face of the invading cohorts of Romans is one which is no longer favoured by modern archaeologists. In only a handful of cases, notably Maiden Castle and Hod Hill in Dorset, have excavations revealed any signs of warfare, such as skeletons and Roman ballista bolts.

I counted over twenty of these places on the map, and in every case they are found on hilltops, spurs or isolated plateaux where they would provide the best possible coigns of vantage for their builders and occupants. The better-known examples include Croft Ambrey, south-west of Ludlow, where hundreds of regularly placed huts have been traced, and Caer Caradoc overlooking the Church Stretton Valley, where Caractacus is said to have made his last stand against the Romans. But there are many more less well known sites. Some, like Burfa Camp, Bury Ditches and Bagbury, are now hidden under

So why were the hillforts built? The answer, as usual in questions about our ancient past, is complex. Some authorities believe that hillforts were the spiritual or religious centres of the Iron Age, and some temples have been found in their interiors. But there is no doubt that many others were settlements, market centres or military installations. In the hill country of the North and West, they may have supported an economy founded on transhumance, serving as summer shielings from which herds of grazing livestock could be watched over a wide area, with the population returning to the less exposed valleys for the winter. But there is also evidence of semi-permanent occupation in many of the Scottish and Welsh forts.

In the softer climate of the South and East, the presence of underground storage pits seems to indicate that the forts were distribution centres for grain and other commodities. Indeed, Professor Barry Cunliffe, the eminent authority on the Iron Age, has suggested that the preponderance of hillforts in the areas where cereal production played an important part in the local economy seems to indicate a fairly stable population. He concluded:

Their very existence implies surplus labour working under coercion, but whether that coercion was the good of the state or the power of a ruling class are matters reserved for more extensive discussion . . .

## Cissbury Ring

Cissbury Ring on the South Downs, overlooks the seaside resort of Worthing in West Sussex. Here the sheep-cropped hilltop has been a place of industry and commerce for at least five thousand years, for, scattered like dimples on the western side of the 20ha (49 acre) fort, are the remains of about 250 neolithic flint mines. Similar to, but less well known than Grimes Graves in the Brecklands of Norfolk, the Cissbury flint mines show up as shallow gorse- and bracken-covered depressions in the butterfly-blessed pastures. From the 12m (40ft) deep bell-shaped mines, the best jet-black flint was mined and later shaped into the delicate flaked axes and

arrowheads which were the height of neolithic technology. Cissbury is one of a chain of hillforts along the South Downs, and excavations have revealed that it was one of the most important. The main rampart still stands 2m (8ft) high in places, and numerous sling stones have been found, indicating that the fort may also have had a defensive function.

In common with many other hillforts, Cissbury had a lengthy period of occupation which extended well into Roman times. During the Roman period, the interior was ploughed up and some small rectangular cottages were built in the enclosed area. The defences were also reinforced late in the Roman period, perhaps as a result of the unrest which marked the departure of the legions.

The ancient name for the fort was Sieberie, and the present name is thought to be the result of sixteenth-century attempts to link it with the Saxon King Cissa. Cissbury shares with many other hillforts along the south coast a local association with Julius Caesar, and in William Camden's *Britannia* of 1695, it is called Caesar's Hill. Centuries ago, ancient remains were almost always attributed to the Romans, a belief which still seems to be current within the Ordnance Survey.

A local legend claims that Cissbury hillfort becomes a dance floor for fairies at midnight on Midsummer's Eve, but the only dancers we saw on our visit were colourful clouds of red admiral, brimstone, chalkhill blue, and meadow brown butterflies. The butterflies were feeding on the numerous vetches, trefoils and bramble bushes on the summit, mimicking the skylarks by spiralling upwards in corkscrews of love as the soaring temperature sparked the mating urge. Everywhere we walked we disturbed drifts of dancing butterflies and an equal number of day-flying burnet moths, smart in vivid scarlet and black. We walked up from the convenient car park in the pretty village of Findon, on the A24 Worthing–Horsham road, and enjoyed a superb picnic on the sunny summit after ritually 'beating the bounds' of the fort and investigating some of the flint-mine hollows.

The views from Cissbury are extensive, to the south over the glittering azure waters of the

Channel, with Worthing and Littlehampton in the foreground. Northwards, they reach to beech-crowned Chanctonbury, and east to Truleigh and Newtimber Hills. Across the prosperous, well-wooded, hedge-and-field landscape of the Sussex barley belt lies the Steyning Gap, created by the River Adur on its journey to the sea.

*Walking the dog on the prehistoric ramparts of Cissbury Ring. This view looks south, towards the genteel holiday resort of Worthing and the waters of the English Channel in the distance. The Ring is a popular resort for residents of Worthing and nearby Brighton, serving a quite different purpose today from that for which it was originally constructed two thousand years ago*

### HAMBLEDON HILL

There is evidence that Hambledon Hill, site of one of the finest hillforts in the south of England just north of Blandford in Dorset, was also occupied in neolithic times. Sharing the sinuous downland ridge with the spectacular, 'contour-type' Iron Age hillfort are the earthworks of three neolithic camps, although, like so many similar downland monuments, they have almost been destroyed by ploughing. Two neolithic long barrows, or burial mounds, also crown the summit of the ridge, 90m (300ft) above the clay valleys of the Rivers Stour and Iwerne.

Hambledon is in many ways a typical large southern hillfort and the result of a long period of

development and occupation. Recent excavations by archaeologist Roger Mercer have demonstrated the part that defence played in maintaining stability in the farming economy of the third millennium BC. Reconstructing the landscape of the times, Mercer has shown that, at the beginning of the period, there were probably three separate enclosures on the airy hilltop of Hambledon. The main enclosure occupied the summit and may have been of ritual significance, possibly used for the excarnation (decomposition by exposure) of bodies before they were buried in the barrows which lay directly north and south. The two other enclosures, one to the south-east and one to the north, may have been settlements

# A Route to Hambledon
## and Hod Hills

The route starts in the strangely named village of Child Okeford, where you take the Steepleton Road past Fernhaynes Copse on the left, with the massive embankments of Hambledon frowning down from the skyline above. Take an obvious chalky cart track to the left, signposted Hambledon Hill, and climb steeply up through beeches to reach a stile with an interpretive plaque. There is a fine view of the sinuous double ramparts of the hillfort from here. The path leads up to the right across ridged sheep pastures, and you should aim for the obvious col between the main hillfort of Hambledon to the left and the earthworks of the neolithic camp to the right.

The views begin to open up now, and it is worth looking back occasionally across the verdant valley of the River Stour to the villages of Shillingstone and Okeford Fitzpaine. At the top of the hill, turn left for a glorious promenade along the mighty ramparts of Hambledon, which sweep majestically around the hilltop, hugging the contours. At the northern end of the fort, the ground drops dramatically away to the farmstead-dotted 'Vale of the Little Dairies' and the downs away to the right, with Melbury Beacon and the hilltop town of Shaftesbury prominent.

Retrace your steps to the central col and the trig point on the neolithic camp. Dropping down to the Cross Dyke, which is now invaded by hawthorns, stick to the ridge path which keeps to the highest point. Eventually, you will descend steeply through Hambledon Plantation past the well-kept Keeper's Lodge. Crossing the Child Okeford–Steepleton road, you bear slightly right to reach the gate which gives access to the National Trust's Hod Hill Estate. Climbing now, you reach a stile with another interpretive board, which gives a brief history of

this fascinating hillfort, at its north-west corner. A circumnavigation of its ramparts reveals a much more regular, straight-sided structure which was in keeping with the imperial style of its last occupants. There are fine views to Steepleton House in the wooded valley of the Iwerne below.

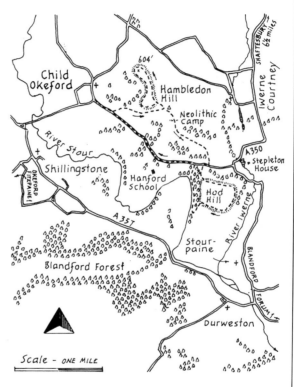

Take the steep path which leads down through thick undergrowth from the south-west corner of the fort to a pleasant, if sometimes muddy, riverside track through Hod Wood. The track leaves the River Stour after about half a mile and climbs up to the Steepleton Road again, just west of Keeper's Lodge. Follow this lane left, past Hansford House School on your left, to re-enter Child Okeford.

either side of the ritual site on the hilltop. Excavations have also revealed flint quarries between the enclosures, and grazing and cultivation may also have taken place here. Earthworks protected the whole hilltop community. The northern end of the present enclosure is still partitioned off by the eroded remains of a bank and ditch, and the southern end of the fort has a similar cross-rampart, separating it from the first main hilltop enclosure. The final Iron Age embankments encompass the whole hill to give it its present size of about 10ha (25 acres).

Aerial photography or, if you are on the hill at the right time, low evening sunlight or a light brushing of snow, reveals a pock-marked interior surface of bumps and hollows. These are the remains of over two hundred mostly circular Iron Age hut platforms, showing that the fort once hosted a sizeable population.

There is no evidence that Hambledon, with its stunning views across the Vale of Blackmoor – Thomas Hardy's 'Vale of the Little Dairies' (see Chapter 5) – to Shaftesbury was ever defended during its Iron Age hey-day. But in the

ABOVE

*Hambledon Hill's enormous hillfort completely dominates the fertile Vale of Blackmoor in this view from the north near Gallow's Corner, close to the hamlet of Fontmell Parva. The builders cleverly utilised the great natural chalk bastion of Hambledon Hill, which forms a prominent outlier of the higher ground of Cranborne Chase to the east, for their impressive fort, which had earlier been the site of a neolithic camp*

OVERLEAF

*Late summer winds bend the seeding grassheads on the western ramparts of Hambledon Hill. Ahead, the sinuous curves of the contour-hugging triple defensive embankments curl around the northern end of the hill, with its breathtaking views across the prosperous villages and farms of Blackmoor Vale*

seventeenth century, it was the scene of the Clubmen's Rising, surely one of the most pathetic incidents of the Civil War. In 1645, sickened by the senseless violence of the internecine strife, a band of 'despairing yokels' led by local church-men armed themselves with clubs, halberds, axes and scythes and determined to stop the fighting by literally banging the opposing factions' heads together. After an initial success which led to the taking of Castle Hill, Shaftesbury, they were driven out by Cromwell's troops to Hambledon for their last stand. By this time, the original 5,000 Clubmen were reduced to about 2,000 red-faced yokels. Cromwell sent out 50 dragoons and, in his own words, 'after a short dispute . . . they beat them from their work, and did some small execution upon them: I believe killed not twelve of them, but cut very many.' Of the dispirited remainder, 300 were imprisoned at Shroton (or Iwerne Courtney) church in the valley below. In a rare act of benevolence, Cromwell wrote to Sir Thomas Fairfax suggesting that these 'poor silly creatures' should be sent home because they had promised 'to be very dutiful for time to come, and will be hanged before they come out again'. So ended the unfortunate Rising of the Clubmen.

A half-mile to the south, just across the minor road between Child Okeford and Steepleton, lies Hod Hill, an equally fascinating hillfort where excavation has shown evidence of a much earlier conflict.

## HOD HILL

Hod Hill is the only example known in this country where an auxiliary Roman fort is super-imposed on an Iron Age hillfort. According to Professor Cunliffe, Hod Hill also provides impressive evidence of pre-Roman occupation with its densely packed circular huts, annexes, enclosures and streets which could have supported a population of up to one thousand people. He believes that the normal population could have been swelled by refugees flooding in from the surrounding countryside in advance of the Roman invaders in the first century, when we know that Vespasian attacked and destroyed twenty such fortified sites in the South West. Dramatic evidence of the Roman attack on Hod Hill in

AD43 was found when archaeologists investigated what was believed to be the chieftain's hut in the south-east sector of the fort. Examination of this hut and its neighbour revealed eleven iron ballista bolts, still embedded in the soil where they had landed from the Roman siege engine, which must have been situated just outside the south-east angle of the fort. As no skeletons or other battle casualties were found, it has been suggested that this demonstration of state-of-the-art military firepower may have been enough to force the Hod Hill garrison to capitulate. After the conquest, the flint breastwork which topped the ramparts was demolished and the 270 or so dwellings inside the fort were destroyed by the Roman troops. Finally stamping their imperial authority on the rebellious tribesmen of Wessex, the Romans constructed their own fort in the north-western corner of the now-derelict Iron Age structure.

The regular defences and playing-card plan of Hod Hill contrast strongly with the gentle, more natural, contour-hugging curves of the earlier work. The views from Hod Hill are magnificent, embracing the winding River Stour which snakes around the peninsula and the curling waves of the chalk downs to the south and east. Ironically, the timber internal buildings of the Roman fort were destroyed by an apparently accidental fire in AD51 – or could it conceivably have been a guerrilla arson attack by those rebellious tribes-men, still smarting from their humiliation eight years before? We will never know.

## MITHER TAP, BENNACHIE

The small but magnificently sited hillfort which crowns the Mither Tap, the easternmost summit of the 5 mile (8km) long Bennachie ridge in Aberdeenshire, may have witnessed the last epic battle of imperial Rome against the Britons. The actual site of the battle in AD84, which the Roman historian Tacitus named Mons Graupius, has been the subject of archaeological debate for many years, but the distinguished Cambridge aerial historian, Professor J. K. St Joseph, has made a strong argument that it took place on the northern slopes of Bennachie. He bases his hypothesis on the proximity of his recent discovery of a large 57ha (140 acre) Roman camp,

just across the River Urie, which flows around the northern foothills of Bennachie. The camp at Durno is in exactly the right position in relation to the string of similar-sized forts constructed by Agricola, who was Tacitus' father-in-law. He was also the subject of Tacitus' eulogistic biography, which documents Agricola's march north to subdue the Caledonians led by Calgacus.

The hillfort on the conical rocky tor of the Mither Tap is in a strong strategic position to overlook the Roman line of advance north from the Firth of Forth. It is linked by a sinuous ridge, nowhere less than 260m (850ft) in height, to the Correen Hills and then to the main mass of the Grampians. And it is the tactical focus of a remarkable concentration of no fewer than six hillforts around Bennachie. Calgacus could not have picked a stronger position from which to defend his mountainous kingdom.

According to Tacitus, Calgacus warned his thirty thousand tribesmen, ranked in close-packed tiers on the steep hillside, of the dire

ABOVE

*The view from the south-western ramparts of Hod Hill, the only known case of an English hillfort being reused by the Romans. The River Stour winds away to the right, with the trees of Blandford Forest topping the rolling Dorset Downs on the horizon. The village of Stourpaine lies away to the left*

OVERLEAF

*A lone walker on the summit of Craigshannoch, a subsidiary top of Bennachie, looks across a now-peaceful scene which may have witnessed a major turning point in British history. The site of the recently discovered Roman camp at Durno lies in the middle distance in this view across the Garioch, the valley of the River Urie. The Roman general Agricola may have used the camp at Durno to embark on his final assault on Calgacus's Caledonians at the Battle of Mons Graupius in AD84, a battle fought out on the slopes of this hill*

consequences of submission to the Romans. 'To robbery, butchery, and rapine, they give the lying name of "government": they create a desolation and call it peace.' Agricola is said to have responded by calling on his Batavians, Tungrians and auxiliaries to: 'Have done with campaigning; crown fifty years with one glorious day, and prove to Rome that her soldiers were never to blame if wars have been allowed to drag on or the seeds of fresh rebellion sowed.'

After an initial exchange of missiles, the Caledonians revealed their tactical naivety by being tempted down from their rocky stronghold into the great natural amphitheatre formed by the northern face of Bennachie. Following an impetuous charge by their fearsome war-chariots,

*The view to the north-west from near the summit of Traprain Law. Like Arthur's Seat and Castle Rock in nearby Edinburgh, Traprain Law is the plug of an extinct volcano, which makes its stone valuable for road building*

they were cut to pieces by the 20,000 strong imperial army. In the terrible slaughter which followed, 10,000 Caledonians were killed, compared to only 360 Roman troops. According to Tacitus, 'Equipment, bodies, and mangled limbs lay all around on the bloodstained earth.' The Battle of Mons Graupius, which Tacitus says took place in the shadow of a hill with *summa collium*, or 'several tops' (a perfect description of Bennachie), saw the end of any further meaningful resistance to the Roman advance, and Agricola returned to Rome triumphant.

Mither Tap and Bennachie are just as prominent landmarks today as they were 1,900 years ago, when they may have witnessed the great turning point in British history which Mons Graupius represents. The long tor-topped ridge is seen from many parts of the rich lowland farming counties of Buchan and Aberdeenshire, and

LEFT _____

*Looking westwards from the commanding rocky summit of Mither Tap, the path leads off through the heather towards Oxen Crag, at 528m (1,732ft), the highest point of the five-mile Bennachie ridge. The ridge leads on to the Correen Hills and Calgacus's apparently impregnable stronghold in the main mass of the Grampians*

*Traprain Law rises like the prow of a great battleship above the green sea of the cereal fields of the Tyne Valley, near East Linton in East Lothian. The much-quarried hill is crowned by the remains of a hillfort which shows a settled and continuous history stretching over a millennium from the Iron Age. Traprain Law is one of a number of prominent hillforts in this part of the Scottish lowlands*

Mither Tap, although lower at 518m (1,698ft), is as obvious a landmark as Schiehallion above Loch Rannoch, or Buachaille Etive Mor at the entrance to Glencoe.

The view from the summit of Mither Tap extends east to the North Sea at Aberdeen, to Lochnagar in the south-west, and the easternmost ramparts of the Cairngorm plateau, with the Ladder Hills and Ben Rinnes to the west. On a clear day, you may even be able to make out the distant mountains of Easter Ross. The usual approach is from Pittodrie or Oyne to the north, crossing the possible area of the battle, or through the gloomy plantations of the Bennachie Forest via Millstone Hill to the south. There are many picnic sites and forest walks in this locally popular weekend retreat for the people of Aberdeen.

### TRAPRAIN LAW

Further south and just across the Forth–Clyde divide is another prominent hill crowned by a fort which has revealed a more peaceful co-existence with the Roman conquerors. Traprain Law is a volcanic plug standing as a northern outlier to the Lammermuir Hills above the valley of the East Lothian River Tyne. It is ringed by a 16ha (40 acre) hillfort which has shown evidence of unbroken occupation for a thousand years, from the end of the Bronze Age to the early Christian era. At least five distinct systems of defence have been discovered by historians. Sadly, in more modern times, the basalt of Traprain Law has been in great demand for road-building, and unsightly quarries now scar its northern end. But archaeologists have uncovered evidence of a peaceful, settled community during the Roman period, including spacious houses, streets, squares and even a stylus, implying that the inhabitants could read and write.

### Tre'r Ceiri

For a taste of what those Iron Age dwellings might have looked like, we must go to the isolated Lleyn Peninsula of North Wales, and the superb viewpoint of Yr Eifl. Usually anglicised to The Rivals (but actually meaning in Welsh 'The Fork') this triple-topped peak has stunning views towards Snowdonia and across the blue waters of Caernarfon Bay to the ancient rocks of Anglesey and the rugged promontory of Holyhead Mountain. Southwards across Cardigan Bay the outline of Mynydd Preseli, source of the Stonehenge bluestones, stands out, and westwards across the Irish Sea, the Wicklow Hills can sometimes be seen.

On a rocky heather-covered plateau below the eastern peak, the substantial remains of some 150 drystone-walled huts, which could have supported a population of 300–400 people, are located within the spectacular hillfort of Tre'r Ceiri. Locally known as the Town of the Giants, Tre'r Ceiri is one of the best preserved of all the hillforts of southern Britain, probably because of its isolation and position 457m (1,500ft) above the sea. In some places, especially on the northern side of the fort, the walls are still nearly 4m (13ft) high, and it is still possible, despite the mindless

---

## A Route to Tre'r Ceiri

There are several paths which lead to this impressive Iron Age city on the triple-topped hill of Yr Eifl, and the most direct for the 'view-bagger' starts from the village of Llanaelhaearn.

Take the B4417 west from the village, past ancient St Aelbaiarn's Well and Uwchlaw'r-ffynnon farmstead on your left. In about three-quarters of a mile you come to a signposted kissing-gate on the right. With the ramparts of Tre'r Ceiri towering above, the path climbs up alongside a wall and through another gate. You now bear left in front of a prominent rocky outcrop to reach the western shoulder of the hill. Here you must keep to the right, where the path from Llithfaen joins from the left. You now climb through the impressive defensive walls of Tre'r Ceiri – 'the town of the giants' – and it is worth spending some time exploring the 150-odd hut foundations to get a true impression of this once-busy township.

From the ancient summit cairn, follow the still impressive 5m (15ft) high north-western rampart to a staggered gateway which passes through both the inner and outer walls. A narrow path threads off to the left, across the thick bushy heather of the col between the east and central summits of Yr Eifl. Follow this path as it climbs steadily to the summit and trig point of the reigning central summit, with its stupendous views. On a clear day, you can easily make out the Wicklow Hills across the Irish Sea. Immediately below to the west is the rocky valley of Nant Gwrtheyrn, named after the fifth-century leader Vortigern who, legend says, had his headquarters here. Having absorbed the breathtaking views, you must turn south, heading towards the distinctive conical hill of Mynydd Carnguwch, crossing a fence and then bearing left by a wall to a stile. Cross the stile and continue downhill to the right to reach the road again, turning left to re-enter Llanaelhaearn.

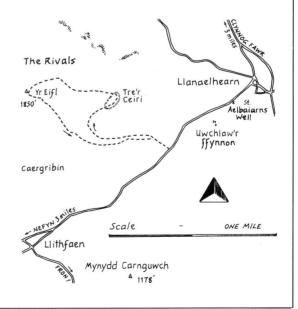

*The summit of Yr Eifl, 564m (1,850ft) on the Lleyn Peninsula, is one of the finest viewpoints in North Wales, combining mountain and seascape in one glorious vista. This is the view looking north-east, towards Gurn Ddu, 522m (1,713ft) in the middle distance, with the distant hills of Snowdonia above that. The Iron Age hillfort town of Tre'r Ceiri lies in the hollow beneath the eastern summit*

stone-throwing activities of some visitors, to walk up the steps or sloping ramps leading up to the original rampart walk of the sentries. The easiest approach to Tre'r Ceiri is from the end of the minor road leading north from the village of Llithfaen. After crossing a level plateau, the track winds steeply up between low tumbled walls to the ruins of the south-west gateway. Only rough grass and bilberries are seen at first, but if you continue up the slope towards the summit, you will encounter groups of small circular huts that appear through the deep heather. Most of these huts have been dated to the fourth century AD, indicating that Tre'r Ceiri was occupied well into the Roman period, as were Cissbury, Hod Hill

and many other hillforts.

Under the encroaching heather, the complete street plan of a native Roman town has been revealed, complete with terraced enclosures which were probably used for cultivation. It would seem that the climate of North Wales was milder during Roman times, for, as Patrick Monkhouse commented in his *On Foot in North Wales* (1934), 'A more cold and cheerless abode I cannot conceive.'

## MAM TOR

Patrick Monkhouse, stylish journalist and champion of the great outdoors, was more generous about Mam Tor, the great 6ha (15 acre) hillfort which completely dominates the Hope Valley in the Derbyshire Peak District. And Mam Tor, at 516m (1,695ft), is even higher than Tre'r Ceiri. But then, for this *Manchester Guardian* man, the Peak was his own country.

In *On Foot in the Peak* (1932), Monkhouse somewhat confusingly describes Mam Tor as 'a gentleman of a hill', for the name is thought to mean 'Mother Mountain'. But he remained open-minded about the earthwork which rings the summit: 'It was here before the Romans came, but whether its purpose was peace or war is a point on which archaeologists differ savagely.'

Since Paddy Monkhouse's day, excavations, notably by Manchester University, have shown that Mam Tor's classic hillfort, one of the most visually impressive in the Pennines, was occupied as early as the late Bronze Age. The balance of archaeological opinion now favours a predominantly peaceful role for the fort and the Brigantian tribesmen who occupied the many excavated hut circles that cover the bald, windswept summit.

Mam Tor was one of Thomas Hobbes' original Seven Wonders of the Peak, first described by him in long-winded Latin verse in 1636, and it has long held a place in local legend. It is popularly known as 'The Shivering Mountain' because of the enormous landslip which scars its eastern face and overlooks Castleton. Mam Tor is built of successive layers of grit and shale which become very unstable after rain and frost, and the 'shiver-ing' epithet refers to its habit of shedding rocks and stones under these conditions. Indeed, the precipitous and highly unstable east face may well have formed an essential part of the defences of the Mam Tor hillfort, for archaeologists now believe that the enormous bank and ditch defences were built up to, and not swept away by, the landslip. The same slow but inexorable forces caused the final abandonment in 1977 of the A625 Castleton–Chapel-en-le-Frith road, which ran directly below the Mam Tor precipice. As a 'Wonder of the Peak,' Mam Tor attracted some of

*The Town of the Giants – Tre'r Ceiri – could have supported a population of 400 people at its height during the Iron Age. The foundations of hut circles such as these in the foreground give a good idea of what life might have been like on this exposed hilltop, 1,500 years ago. Bilberry and heather are encroaching now, but it is still possible to imagine the circular huts with their thatched roofs populated by local tribespeople. This view looks south-west down the peninsula*

# A Route to Mam Tor

The Mam Tor–Lose Hill ridge walk is the finest in the Peak – an area not well blessed with ridge routes. The more experienced walker may wish to use the 2 mile (3km) ridge as part of the more ambitious 26 mile (42km) Edale Skyline walk which encompasses the highest points that may be seen from the green valley nestling at the foot of Kinder Scout. However, most family ramblers will be content with the easy and popular stroll across the tops of Mam Tor, Back Tor and Lose Hill, perhaps returning by a valley route to take in the tourist attractions of Castleton, with its castle and caverns.

Using the National Park car park just below Mam Nick, walk up the wooden staircase through the trees to reach the stile at the top of the road, where it drops down into Edale. A well-constructed stone stairway, made by National Trust volunteers, leads up through the ramparts and onto the summit of Mam Tor, which is one of the most impressive hillforts in the Pennines. Do not stray too close to the precipitous east face, which gives the hill its alternative name of the Shivering Mountain. The alternating bands of shale and grit are extremely loose and dangerous, and even experienced climbers will not venture on it unless it is frozen solid in winter. After admiring the wonderful view, turn east and walk along the heavily eroded path – an indication of its popularity – through the ramparts again and down to the col of Hollins Cross, where the dead from Edale were once carried across to Castleton for burial.

Mounting Barker Bank, you start the steep ascent of Back Tor, with its crumbling face of shale and grit, which faces Edale and the north. The ridge continues more gently to reach the shapely summit of Lose Hill, which is more correctly known as Ward's Piece in memory of G. H. B. 'Bert' Ward, the king of the Sheffield-based Clarion Ramblers. Ward was an indefatigable fighter for access on these Peak moors, and his pragmatic motto was: 'A man who never was lost, never went very far.' Field paths lead down to Castleton via Losehill Farm and Fields Farm, and you can return to your car at Mam Nick either by the impressive limestone gorge of the Winnats ('wind gates') Pass, or by following the now closed A625 road, which was finally swept away by the almost continuous landslips from Mam Tor.

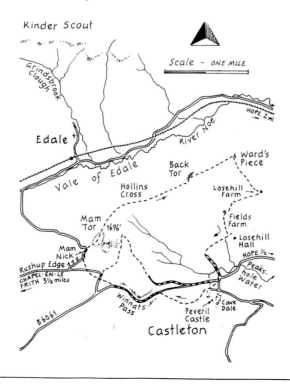

the earliest tourists to this popular area, including Celia Fiennes, who described it in her journey through Britain in the reign of William and Mary as being 'all broken that it looks just in resemblance as a great Hay-Ricke thats cut down one halfe'. A few years later, Daniel Defoe in his *Tour Through the Whole Island of Great Britain* was more dismissive, especially about the legend that although Mam Tor is constantly being washed away, it never seems to get smaller. 'Nothing is more certain than this,' he wrote, 'that the more water comes down from it, the less remains in it; and so it certainly is of Mam Tor, in spite of all the poetry of . . . Mr Hobbes, and in spite of all the women's tales in the Peak.'

Mam Tor, now owned and protected by the National Trust, is easily approached from the National Park car park just below the col of Mam Nick, where a minor road winds steeply down into Edale. It also forms a terminus of the finest

*Rain clouds threaten in this view down the verdant Hope Valley from Mam Tor. The curiously contorted landscape directly below the viewpoint is caused by the unstable shales of the mountain, which is constantly subject to landslips. These were the cause in 1977 of the final closure of the main Castleton to Chapel-en-le-Frith road which ran directly beneath, after many years of very expensive but ultimately futile repairs by the highway authority*

ridgewalk in the Peak, for the Mam Tor–Lose Hill ridge effectively separates the White Peak (limestone) from the Dark Peak (gritstone), with splendid panoramas on all sides.

The views from Mam Tor are justly famous: to the north, across the green vale of Edale threaded by the railway line, to the frowning plateau of Kinder Scout with Grindsbrook Booth village nestling at its feet. Eastwards is the long tor-topped line of Derwent Edge and the Eastern

ABOVE

*The great 'layer-cake' east face of Mam Tor, as seen from above Odin Mine on Treak Cliff, near Castleton in the Peak District. This crumbling face gave Mam Tor the nickname of The Shivering Mountain, and it may have been used as part of the defences of the extensive hillfort which crowns the 516m (1,695ft) summit*

RIGHT

*An unusual view of Ingleborough's fort-topped summit, as seen from the north-west above the limestone pavements of Twistleton Scar on the edge of Scales Moor above Chapel le Dale. The sloping parallel pavements of Raven Scar are seen across the deep Chapel Beck valley in the middle distance. In the foreground, early purple orchids make a fine show as they enjoy the lime-rich pastures with the rank moor grass*

*Ingleborough's bald summit, as seen from the peaty springs which dot the southern shoulder of Little Ingleborough, above Clapham in the Yorkshire Dales. This is the usual approach for walkers ascending the mountain from Clapham to the south via Clapham Beck, Trow Gill and Gaping Gill – the largest open pothole in Britain. By this stage of the walk, you have left the limestone behind, and are on the gritstone cap which crowns the hill*

Moors, with the shapely cone of Lose Hill and the sharp pike of Win Hill prominent. Looking south, the 300m (1,000ft) White Peak plateau forms the skyline and the hawthorn-hedged Hope Valley is spread out at your feet punctuated by the white cement works chimney at Hope. Looking slightly west, the deep gash of Winnats Pass, which now takes the Chapel road, can just be seen. Castleton village is just across the valley and the gorge of Peak Cavern with, as Paddy Monkhouse perfectly described it, 'the keep of Peveril Castle standing on the edge of it like a lump of sugar balanced on a dog's nose'.

## INGLEBOROUGH

Another headquarters of the Brigantes, and one which some imaginative historians have claimed was the last stronghold of their leader Venutious against the invading Romans, is Ingleborough, one of the Yorkshire Dales' famed Three Peaks. Indeed, one author has gone even further and likened the 6ha (15 acre) hillfort whose broken walls ring the 723m (2,372ft) summit to Masada, the Dead Sea fortress where an army of fanatical Jews commited mass suicide rather than submit to the Romans.

In fact, there is no evidence of a battle or even of a siege on Ingleborough, apart from the continuing uphill battle of the National Park authority to try to keep pace with the footpath repairs that are needed in the wake of the 120,000 pairs of ramblers' boots which annually lay siege to this most popular Yorkshire summit. It is said that every Yorkshireman must climb Ingleborough at least one in his life, and the popularity of the 24 mile (39km) Three Peaks challenge walk has added immensely to this locally generated

# A Route to Ingleborough

Park in the National Park car park in Clapham village, then turn right along the village street and cross the charming stone footbridge over Clapham Beck. Follow the beck upstream through the woodyard of the Ingleborough Estate, where a small charge is made for the walk through the beautifully landscaped grounds. Passing the large artificial lake and an ugly grotto in the ornamental woodlands, you emerge at a stile by Clapdale Beck and the water pump which feeds Clapdale Farm above to the left. The dale narrows as it approaches the mouth of Ingleborough Cave which, having been opened in 1837, is the oldest show cave in the area. Beyond Beck Head the dale is dry, and as it bends to the left, you cross a stile to enter the dramatic little limestone ravine of Trow Gill which was formed by the meltwaters of an Ice Age glacier. Scramble out of the boulder choke at the head of Trow Gill and over a stile which leads out onto the open moor known as Clapham Bottom. A well-trodden path leads north-west past the mouths of several sealed-off potholes towards the wire fence which sur-rounds the greatest of them all – Gaping Gill. Some 111m (365ft) deep and big enough to hold the nave of York Minster, Gaping Gill is the largest open pothole in Britain.

Our route continues north-west across the boggy moor to reach the shoulder of the hill ahead, which is known as Little Ingleborough. Pick your way right, through the crags and loose stones of the ancient fortifications to reach the broad summit plateau of Ingleborough itself, with its prominent summit shelter and trig point. Return the way you came as far as the cairn on Little Ingleborough, then descend quite steeply south-south-west across the rough moorland of Newby Moss. Eventually, you will pick up the shallow valley of Grey Wife Syke, with the village of Newby directly ahead. Entering up a green lane, you emerge past an old quarry at the seventeenth-century farmstead of Newby Cote. Turn left along this quiet lane, which was once the main highway between Leeds and Kendal, to reach Clapham again in just over a mile.

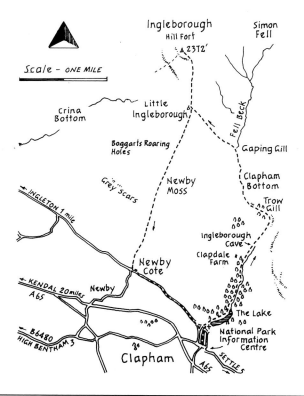

111

traffic. For this reason I hesitate to include Ingleborough in our list of viewpoints, but it is the highest hillfort in Britain, and the panorama from its bald flat summit is so good that it cannot be ignored.

The bold stepped profile of Ingleborough imposes itself on the whole of Three Peak country, and is caused by the underlying geology which has left a cap of Yoredale series millstone grits, shales and sandstones resting on the bedrock of Carboniferous limestone. Below Ingleborough's summit the country is hollow, with some of Britain's largest and deepest pot-holes. The awesome, yawning chasm of Gaping Gill on the mountain's southern flank is the grandfather of them all.

On the western and eastern sides of Ingleborough, extensive areas of gleaming white limestone pavement, fretted with clints and grikes, show the abrasive passage of Ice Age glaciers which scraped the surface soil and vegetation clear. There are four main routes to the summit, from Clapham, Ingleton, Chapel-le-Dale and Selside, but whichever route you choose, it is unlikely that you will have the spacious summit to yourself on such a popular hill.

The view from the slightly cluttered summit, with a cross-wall wind shelter (the view indicator at its centre was erected to mark the Coronation in 1953), various cairns and the fragmentary remains of some hut circles, is justly famous. It is especially good looking north, across Chapel Dale to the cloud-dappled hump of Whernside, and west, where, on a clear day, you can just make out the distinctive thimble-like summits of the Langdale Pikes in the Lake District and the shining waters of Morecambe Bay. Looking east, the silvery limestone pavements of Sulber and Moughton flank Ribblesdale, with the crouching lion of Pen-y-ghent, the third of the Three Peaks, beyond.

## THE BRITISH CAMP, MALVERN HILLS

When William Langland dreamed of 'A faire felde of folk' from the Malvern Hills one bright May morning some time during the fourteenth century, he was creating perhaps the greatest English poem of the Middle Ages. It was certainly one of the most popular, for over fifty manuscripts still survive. This impressive miniature range of hills that forms the border between the old counties of Herefordshire and Worcestershire always seem to have had the ability to inspire people. Six centuries later, they were to provide the same kind of inspiration for Edward Elgar, who was born in their shadow, to write some of the finest supremely English music of our times. He once said: 'If ever you're walking on the hills and hear my Cello Concerto, don't be frightened, it's only me.' Everest mountaineer Wilfred Noyce reckoned that of all the British ranges, the ancient pre-Cambrian rocks of the Malvern Hills came nearest to the Himalaya in the way they rise so suddenly and steeply out of the surrounding plain. It is not surprising, therefore, that the Herefordshire Beacon at the southern end of the hills attracted our Iron Age predecessors as a suitable site for one of the most impressive of their hillforts.

Popularly known as the British Camp, and with a pub named after it in the col below where the Malvern to Ledbury road crosses the range, this 340m (1,114ft) summit is crowned by the beautifully sinuous curving earthworks of a 13ha (32 acre) contour-type hillfort. Legend says that this could be the site where Caractacus fought his last battle against the Romans before he was captured and taken to Rome, a tradition which the Herefordshire Beacon shares with Caer Caradoc in Shropshire.

At the centre and on the highest point of the fort, there is a later Norman motte-and-bailey earthwork, known as The Citadel. Excavations have shown that this was a minor castle during the twelfth century, probably in defence against

RIGHT _____

*Looking south in late evening sun from the so-called British Camp, which crowns the 340m (1,114ft) summit of the Herefordshire Beacon in the delectable Malvern Hills. The great sweeping embankments of the hillfort can be seen directly above the figure to the right, while the view south takes in Broad Down and Hangman's Hill and across the Severn Plain beyond. The actual summit is marked by a Norman motte-and-bailey earthwork, known as The Citadel*

# THE MALVERN RIDGE

Regular rail travellers on the main cross-country route between the North East and the South West look forward to seeing the shapely long blue outline of the Malvern Hills as they speed south down the Severn Valley. Looking like a sleeping dragon, the Malverns are the first hint after the broad green acres of the Midlands that the greater hills of the West and Wales are at hand. This is soon confirmed by the green slopes of Bredon Hill and the first of the Cotswolds which close in to the east.

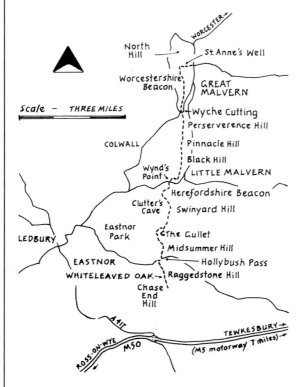

But, as Everest mountaineer Wilfred Noyce pointed out, despite their modest height the Malverns give a wonderful impression of a real mountain range, especially when they are dusted with winter snow. The 10 mile (16km) traverse of the entire Malvern ridge is one of the finest walks in the Midlands, with stunning views on all sides, and is best started from the northern end and the pleasant spa town of Great Malvern.

Walk up past St Ann's Well, Malvern's most

famous spring of pure water and celebrated in the doggerel verse:

The Malvern Water, says Dr John Wall,
Is famed for containing just nothing at all.

A broad tarmaced track with convenient seats gives access to Green Valley, now known as Happy Valley, and the col between North Hill, to the right, and the reigning summit of the Worcestershire Beacon 422m (1,385ft). The toposcope here shows that, in the right conditions, the cathedrals of Worcester, Gloucester and Hereford can be seen. Hay Bluff in the Black Mountains is to the west, while Shropshire's Clee Hills and the Wrekin are due north. A café is open here during the season.

Easy paths, constructed and maintained by the venerable Malvern Hills Conservators, lead down to the Wyche Cutting, one of the oldest of the passes over the hills and the route of an ancient Saltway between the Severn and Herefordshire. Parallel paths lead up over the aptly named Perseverance Hill, or you can take the engineered Jubilee Drive on the western side, with excellent views into the well-wooded border countryside of Herefordshire. The track contours under Pinnacle and Black Hill to reach the next major pass through the hills at Wynds Point. Wynds Point, and the British Camp public house, is a popular starting point for the ascent of the Herefordshire Beacon, otherwise known as the British Camp, with the wonderful contour-type hillfort ringing its summit.

Past Clutter's Cave the paths follow Red Earl's Dyke, an ancient boundary ditch, mounting Swinyard Hill before they drop down to the Gullet, with its unsightly quarry. The Conservators were formed in 1884 primarily to stop such quarries eating away at the distinctive outline of the Malvern Hills, and overall they have done a fine job in protecting the hills so that future generations may enjoy them.

Midsummer Hill, the next major summit, is occupied by another Iron Age hillfort, although at 11ha (27 acres), it is nowhere near as extensive as that which crowns the Herefordshire Beacon. The medieval 'pillow mounds' on Hollybush Hill were constructed to encourage rabbits to breed when they were an important source of fresh meat. The Red Earl's Dyke leads down to the Golden Valley and Hollybush, where the A438 Tewkesbury–Hereford road crosses the hills.

According to legend, a curse will fall on anyone who passes within the shadow of Raggedstone Hill, the next summit. The story is that a monk from Little Malvern Priory fell in love with a local girl and, having been discovered by the prior, his punishment was to crawl on his hands and knees daily to the top of Raggedstone Hill. One day, instead of praying when he reached the top, he cursed the hill and anyone on whom its shadow might fall. One suspects he might have had the prior particularly in mind.

At one time the three ancient counties of Herefordshire, Worcestershire and Gloucestershire met at the tiny hamlet of Whiteleaved Oak, which you pass as you cross a lane to mount the most southerly of the Malvern range, Chase End Hill. This final summit overlooks the scar of the M50 Ross Spur motorway and gives tempting distant views of the Black Mountains beyond Hereford.

*The long line of the Malvern Hills ridge as seen from the ramparts of the British Camp. The wooded slopes of the Herefordshire side of the hills is well shown, as is the line of the Jubilee Drive, constructed to celebrate the Jubilee of Queen Victoria in 1887, winding below the summits of Black Hill and Pinnacle Hill, with the Worcestershire Beacon beyond*

Welsh incursions, much like the Shropshire examples mentioned earlier.

Also of this period is the so-called Red Earl's Dyke, or Shire Ditch, which runs from near the southern end of the fort for about 1½ miles (2.4km) to Midsummer Hill to the south. This was built by Gilbert de Clare, Earl of Gloucester, in about 1287 to define his hunting land of Malvern Chase from the land of the Bishop of Hereford. He cunningly built it just below the ridge so that the Bishop's deer could easily jump over it but not jump back.

The British Camp has received the attention of generations of archaeologists, professional and amateur, who have estimated that the final hill-fort could have housed a population of between 1,500 and 2,000 in small rectangular wooden huts spread across the low terraces of the interior. Like many similar hillforts, it lacks a permanent water supply, so supplies of Iron Age 'Malvern water' must have been taken from nearby springs in the hillside. Another Iron Age hillfort crowns Mid-summer Hill to the south.

Like the Shropshire hills further north, the Malverns stand on the border between upland and lowland Britain, and the views from the Here-fordshire Beacon illustrate this. On a clear day, it seems as if you are looking straight into the heart of rural England. Looking east, across the rich well-wooded plain of the lower Severn, Bredon Hill lies in front of the long blue skyline which marks the Cotswolds. Southwards, the silvery glint of the Severn Estuary can sometimes be seen, while to the west, the more broken land of the Welsh Marches, with the Black Mountains and Brecon Beacons beyond, is spread out before you. Looking north, the foreground is filled by the shaggy western slopes of the Malverns, their bald summits (the name comes from the Welsh, moel bryn–'bald hill') stretching enticingly, like a roller-coaster, to the reigning summit of the Worcestershire Beacon over 5 miles (8km) away.

The Malverns make a fine ridge walk at any time of the year, and are thankfully protected by the Malvern Hills Conservators, founded by special act of parliament in 1884 as one of the earliest area conservation bodies in the country.

About 180m (200yd) to the south-east of the Herefordshire Beacon, a small man-made cave known as Giant's or Clutter's Cave is said to have been the home of a hermit in the Middle Ages. It illustrates once more how local people often used legendary beings to explain the apparently in-explicable.

## WANDLEBURY

Across on the other side of the country, among the flat fens and enormous skies of East Anglia, a similar device was used to describe the low chalky ridge which rises abruptly to the south-east of the university city of Cambridge. This now well-wooded eminence just off the Cambridge–Colchester road has been known for generations as the Gog Magog Hills. Prince Gog and the land of Magog were first mentioned by the prophet Ezekiel in the Old Testament. In the twelfth century, the names were united by Geoffrey of Monmouth, who claimed that Gogmagog was a mythical giant who fought a battle with the Britons before he was killed by the Trojan general Corineus. There are statues apparently represent-ing Gog and Magog, last of the British giants, in London's Guildhall.

Crowning the chalky spur of Cambridgeshire's Gog Magog Hills is the Iron Age hillfort of Wandlebury, once a stronghold of Boudicca's Iceni and now partly overlaid by the eighteenth-century home and grounds of Lord Godolphin. It is now a country park and a popular playground for the people of Cambridge. Although only just over 90m (300ft) above the sea, its situation above the low-lying prairie lands of the fens means that long distances are visible, as far as the towers of Ely Cathedral, 20 miles (32km) to the north, and across the spires and minarets of Cambridge itself. The chalky ramparts of Wandlebury hillfort were the scene of one of the most sensational dis-coveries, or elaborate hoaxes, in the world of archaeology in the 1950s. T. C. Lethbridge, one of the most colourful characters in British archaeology and a distinguished Anglo-Saxon scholar at the University of Cambridge, claimed that he had discovered an elaborate tableau of hill figures at Wandlebury which were unlike any others previously found in Britain. They seemed to show giants, goddesses, and a beaked horse and chariot. Lethbridge claimed that they showed that the ancient name of the hills was based on the hill carving of the giants. However, his methodology and single-minded determination to prove his dubious theories were dismissed by other archaeologists, although they were welcomed by the so-called lunatic fringe. Lethbridge's theory was based on the well-documented probability that a hill figure did once exist on the slopes of Wandlebury. From the early seventeenth century, there are reports of the scholars of Cambridge cutting a hill figure out of the turf of the hill.

The Cambridge antiquarian John Layer wrote in 1640 that he could not understand how the hills got their name

> unless it were from a high and mighty portraiture of a giant wch the schollars of Cambridge cut upon the turf or superficies of earth within the said trench, and not unlikely might call it Gogmagog, which I have seen but it is now of late discontinued

It was also recalled by the Birmingham antiquarian William Cole in about 1724, but none of the many amateur antiquarians of the last century seem to have mentioned it, or to have thought it worth investigating.

Whatever the truth, the strange 'buried gods' which T. C. Lethbridge uncovered in the 1950s are now overgrown and only barely visible from the air. And Wandlebury hillfort, although still impressive, has been extensively modified by the landscaping and tree planting of the grounds of Lord Godolphin's eighteenth-century mansion. The inner of the two large banks and ditches was levelled when the grounds were laid out, but excavations have revealed that storage pits and the post holes of rectangular buildings once existed in the interior of the 6ha (15 acre) fort.

Local legend claims that those last two British giants, Gog and Magog, still lie buried under the chalk slopes of Wandlebury. Maybe one day they will surface less controversially than they did in the 1950s, when they raised so much heat and dust in the world of archaeology.

---

## East Anglian Views

Each region of Britain has its special features which distinguish it from the rest. In the Pennines, it is the rugged moors and miles of drystone walls; the Lake District has its softly romantic lakes and fells; while Warwickshire and the West Midlands have the most stately trees, living reminders of Shakespeare's Arden.

The attraction of East Anglia is in its stupendous and all-embracing skies. There are no dawns like those over the Suffolk or North Norfolk coasts, and no sunsets like those which tint the ruler-straight dykes of the shimmering Fens. With this wonderful clarity of air, it is no coincidence that the region has attracted so many of our finest artists, from John Constable to Thomas Gainsborough. As Constable himself wrote:

> Painting for me is another word for feeling, and I associate my careless boy-hood with all that lies on the banks of the Stour; those scenes made me a painter. As long as I am able to hold a brush, I shall never cease to paint them.

So what East Anglia may lack in outstanding physical viewpoints, it more than makes up for in its superb skyscapes. In a single summer afternoon, you can see a gathering storm with the towering black anvils of thunder clouds in one quarter, with a dazzling rainbow in their vanguard; and in the other, the sky will be that piercing cobalt blue which lights up the seemingly endless prairies of gently swaying wheat with an eye-blinking intensity. Those bubbling clouds and spectacular sunsets were a boon for a hill-seeker like me, born and brought up in the flatness of the Essex–Suffolk border, for I would imagine all sorts of mountains and lakes in those ever-changing skies.

FACTBOX

| | GR | MAP |
|---|---|---|
| Croft Ambrey, Shropshire | SO445668 | LR137 Ludlow & Wenlock Edge |
| Caer Caradoc, Shropshire | SO476955 | LR137 Ludlow & Wenlock Edge |
| Cissbury Ring, Sussex | TQ139080 | LR198 Brighton & The Downs |
| Hambledon Hill, Dorset | ST844128 | LR194 Dorchester & Weymouth |
| Hod Hill, Dorset | ST857106 | LR194 Dorchester & Weymouth |
| Mither Tap, Bennachie | NJ682224 | LR38 Aberdeen |
| Traprain Law, East Lothian | NT581746 | LR67 Duns, Dunbar & Eyemouth |
| Tre'r Ceiri, The Rivals | SH373446 | LR123 Lleyn Peninsula |
| Mam Tor, Derbyshire | SK128838 | OL1 Dark Peak |
| Ingleborough, North Yorkshire | SD741747 | OL2 Yorkshire Dales – Western |
| British Camp, Malvern Hills | SO760400 | LR150 Worcester & The Malverns |
| Wandlebury Camp, Cambridge | TL493534 | LR154 Cambridge & Newmarket |

# 4
# MONUMENTAL
# VIEWPOINTS

Hill figures like the 'buried gods' of the Gog Magog Hills are a peculiarly English phenomenon, relying almost exclusively on the unique, smooth, sheep-cropped chalk downlands of the South and West for their canvas. Here there is mile after mile of steep green slopes and smooth escarpments where the turf artist can exercise his ancient skill to perfection. The comparatively easy removal of the thin skin of downland turf reveals the dazzling white chalk instantly, and the rolling landscape itself, full of inviting ridges and grand vistas, seems made for what one authority has dubbed 'leucippotomy' – the cutting of white horses. All but four of the English hill figures are found in the chalk country of the downs, and of the seventeen white horses – easily the most popular subject – eleven are found within the ancient kingdom of Wessex.

There are other subjects, of course, like the two surviving giants, the Long Man of Wilmington and the splendidly uninhibited 'ithyphallic and clavigerous' Cerne Abbas Giant; one or two white crosses and a number of modern figures, such as the Whipsnade Lion, the Bulford Kiwi and the regimental badges at Fovant Down on the southern edge of Salisbury Plain. But the classic hill figure is that of a horse, and the prototype of the genre, and undoubtedly the earliest example, is the mysterious, dragon-like creature which still gallops across the edge of the downs at Uffington in Berkshire.

The Uffington White Horse is thought to have been made as a totem for the early tribespeople who inhabited the area and who were probably also responsible for the construction of the hill-fort of Uffington Castle, which occupies the summit of the hill above. In other words, it was a sort of Iron Age regimental badge, made for much the same reasons as those created by World War I soldiers at Fovant.

Horses of similar design are found on Iron Age coins and it is believed that the Uffington horse was cut in order to reinforce the identity of the tribe and to advertise its presence to outsiders.

The Uffington horse is undoubtedly very ancient, having been first recorded soon after the Norman Conquest. One or two of the other white horse figures, according to some authorities, may originally have been cut in celebration of Saxon victories over the invading Danes. But the vast majority of the white horse hill figures appear to have been cut during the seventeenth, eighteenth and nineteenth centuries, apparently at the whim of local landowners. Several reasons have been given for this practice, including antiquarian interest in the Uffington figure, the growth of landscaping, and the popularity of horse portraits and engravings, inspired, perhaps, by the fashionable work of George Stubbs (1724–1806). White horses share with other follies, sham ruins and prospect towers the common tale that they were constructed at a time of severe unemployment, on the instruction of a public-spirited landlord who wanted to find his men something 'useful' to do. Most of these stories, on investigation, seem to have emanated from the 'benefactors' themselves, so perhaps should be treated with a degree of scepticism.

The growth in appreciation of romantic, or picturesque, scenery in the eighteenth or nine-

teenth centuries created an impulse among landowners to want to try to 'improve' it by the addition of prospect towers and artificial ruins. The prospect towers, such as that on the Cotswold edge at Broadway, were set up in situations where they could command the prospect of distant views. The eighteenth-century poet, James Thomson, expressed this desire in his poem 'The Seasons':

> Heav'ns, what a goodly prospect spreads
>    around,
> Of hills, and dales, and woods, and lawns,
>    and spires!
> And glittering towns, and gilded streams, till all
> The stretching landskip into smoke decays.

'Landskip' was the Dutch word for landscape, and was first made popular by Milton in his poem 'L'Allegro'. Sham ruins, such as that at Mow Cop and McCaig's Folly at Oban were copied from classic continental paintings, which often featured a ruined tower in their composition. They were designed to add medieval or Gothic interest to a landscape, to draw the eye and hold it there. They often carried overtones of chivalry, or may even have been attempts to make a moral point on the transience of earthly values. Monuments, on the other hand, were generally set up in celebration of a local or national hero or event, or simply for the self-aggrandisement of the builder.

One thing that all these monumental structures – these 'Eyeful Towers' – have in common, from the white horses to obelisks and from towers to sham ruins, was that they were made to be seen, and therefore without exception they were placed on prominent viewpoints. Some also

*A classic view of Hadrian's Wall, from above Cuddy's Crags looking east along the line of the wall towards the tree-topped Housesteads Crag and the distant Sewing-shields Crag, above Broomlee Lough. Only by walking the wall can you share the feelings which the legionaries must have felt when they were posted to this bleak and inhospitable outpost of their empire. They must have been similar to those experienced by a German soldier being posted to the Russian Front during World War II*

doubled as beacons, to be lit in time of national celebration or emergency, such as to warn the population of an impending invasion. Lord Macaulay's poem on the approaching Armada four hundred years ago graphically illustrates the power of this fiery form of communication, and, incidentally, links several of the viewpoints we visit in this book:

> All night from tower to tower they sprang,
>    they sprang from hill to hill;
> Till the proud Peak unfurled the flag o'er
>    Darwin's (Derwent's) rocky dales,
> Till like volcanoes flared to heaven the stormy
>    hills of Wales,
> Till twelve fair counties saw the blaze on
>    Malvern's lonely height,
> Till streamed in crimson on the wind the
>    Wrekin's crest of light . . .

## HADRIAN'S WALL

There are few ancient man-made structures in Britain which are visible from satellites, but one is the 73 mile (117km) wall that was erected across the neck of Britain on the orders of the Emperor Hadrian in AD122. Following the natural escarpment of the Great Whin Sill (see Chapter 1), Hadrian's Wall was the northernmost limit of the Roman Empire – the very edge of civilisation in those days. Today, it provides a superb, mainly high-level walk across Britain, with stunning views, and its attraction was officially recognised recently when the Countryside Commission proposed it as a new long-distance trail.

The man who first claimed to have walked the length of Hadrian's Wall was William Hutton who, in 1801, at the age of 78, walked the 600 miles (965km) from Birmingham to the Wall, along its entire length, and back to Birmingham in 35 days. Hutton was a businessman and antiquarian, and his boast that 'Perhaps I am the first man that ever walked the whole length of this wall and probably the last that will ever attempt it' is likely to be proved wrong in a bigger way than he could ever have imagined when the new 'Hadrian's Way' is inaugurated.

The wall has held a magnetic attraction for antiquarians for generations. In *Puck of Pook's Hill*,

Rudyard Kipling used the dedicated centurion Parnesius to impart some of the end-of-the-world feelings which Roman legionaries must have felt when they were posted to this last outpost of the empire.

> Just when you think you are at the world's end, you see a smoke from East to West as far as the eye can turn, and then, under it, also as far as the eye can stretch, houses and temples, shops and theatres, barracks and granaries, trickling along like dice behind – always behind – one long, low, rising and falling, and hiding and showing line of towers. And that is the Wall!

Jessie Mothersole, guidebook author and artist, was quite simply in love with the wall. In her *Hadrian's Wall* (1922) – incidentally still one of the most charming companions to a walk along the wall – she enthuses:

> I love the Wall because I can picture it, manned by the soldiers of the cohorts, as a living thing, all eyes and ears; a link from sea to sea; a chain of forts and turrets threaded on a single string!

According to his biographer, Hadrian constructed the wall 'to separate the Romans from the barbarians'. And for nearly four hundred years, it stood as a permanent and obvious frontier, 3m (10ft) thick and 4.5m (15ft) high, stretching from Tynemouth to the Solway Firth, punctuated by milecastles and turrets and supported by forts such as those at Housesteads and Chesters. These military structures were backed by the earthworks of the Vallum which barred entry from the south into the 'frontier zone'.

The magic of the wall remains, for, despite the attentions of local developers who for centuries used it as a quarry for building stone, it is still the most important surviving memorial to the military power of the Roman Empire. There is nothing else like it in Europe, and the finest way to appreciate the enormity of Hadrian's concept is to follow in the footsteps of the cohorts and walk along it.

Probably the best section of the wall for the view-seeker is the spectacular stretch between Housesteads and Crag Lough which passes over the natural defensive roller-coaster of the Great Whin Sill and takes in the finest surviving fort at Housesteads. A little further to the east, the wall mounts Sewingshields Crag which, as mentioned in Chapter 2, is one of the many legendary sites of King Arthur's eternal vigil. But we will start our walk at Housesteads, probably the best-preserved Roman fort in Europe, and the biggest single attraction on the wall since the eighteenth century.

It is the small details which have survived in places like Housesteads which bring Roman Britain to life. Preserved in the grey sandstone are such domestic details as the legionaries' lavatories and the worn-down ruts created by Roman carts in the stones of the main eastern gateway. Their 'gauge' of 4ft 8½in is exactly that chosen by George Stephenson for our modern railways – yet another example of our debt to pioneering Roman technology.

Walking west from Housesteads, occupied in the fifth century by the 1st Cohort of Tungrians and later probably by locally enlisted auxiliaries, the wall climbs the steep escarpment of the Whin Sill. It is known here as Cuddy's Crags, a name which derives from the local nickname of the popular misogynist Northumbrian saint, Cuthbert.

Within half a mile, Housesteads milecastle, one of the best preserved, is passed. An inscribed stone found here recorded the fact that it was built by the Second Legion under the governorship of Aulus Platorius Nepos, the man Hadrian had appointed to build the wall.

RIGHT _____

*The Roman fort of Housesteads on Hadrian's Wall is among the best preserved in Britain, a fact which must have something to do with its isolation. The Roman name of Vercovicium (meaning hilly place) seems to bear this out, but it was garrisoned by one thousand infantry soldiers, later reinforced by cavalry. It was built to defend incursions along the Knag Burn. Much of the present remains date from the third and fourth centuries, and include a headquarters building, commander's house, barracks, bath houses, latrines, workshops, hospital and granaries. A vicus, or civil settlement, has been identified to the south*

# A WALK ALONG THE WALL

Even after 1,800 years, Hadrian's Wall from the Solway to Tyneside remains Europe's finest monument to Rome's military might. News that the Countryside Commission intend to make the 73 mile (117km) route a national long-distance trail will undoubtedly result in many more people coming to know it and the many fine viewpoints which are available to the wall-walker.

In this chapter, we have visited a couple of the best-known viewpoints at Housesteads and Cuddy's Crags, but a walk along the wall, as authors from William Hutton to Jessie Mothersole and Hunter Davies have described, is a constant journey of discovery. Leaving the industrial suburbs of Newcastle-upon-Tyne, where the district of Wallsend means exactly what it says, the first real high point is Rudchester (Vindobala) Roman fort, with a commanding view over the Tyne valley to the south. Halton Chester fort (Onnvm) was a large fort garrisoned by five hundred soldiers. A few miles to the south, Corbridge (Corstopitum) guarded the crossing of Dere Street over the Tyne, and is now the site of an interesting museum of finds from the wall.

Marching west, the visible remains of the wall become more obvious, until at Chesters the extensive remains of a bridge abutment over the River North Tyne can be seen below the large fort of Cilurnum, where there is another fascinating museum. The views from the river of the Cilurnum bath house are particularly fine and prompted Jessie Mothersole to produce several paintings. You are now entering high country, and the views of and from the wall open up as it climbs Walwick Fell.

Milecastle 30, usually known as Limestone Corner, is the northernmost point of the wall, and provides magnificent views of the Cheviots to the north and the valley of the South Tyne in the opposite direction. Carrawburgh fort (Brocolitia) guarded the Newbrough Burn and North Tynedale. The B6318, which follows General Wade's military road built in the 1740s on the foundations of the wall, is now left behind as the wall strides purposefully towards the high point of Sewingshields Crag, another fine viewpoint.

You are now on the best-preserved area of the wall, a fact that is probably due to its isolation on the high Whin Sill escarpment.

The well-preserved wall climbs through straggling pines above the still dark waters of Crag Lough, perhaps one of the most beautiful of the Northumbrian lakes. The steep dolerite crags of Hotbank Crags below you to the right provided a superb natural defence for the Roman engineers, while today they provide many challenging routes for the rock climber, with aptly named routes like the Appian Way. Crag Lough is still the home of water-lilies and wildfowl, just as it must have been when Tungrian legionaries patrolled this section of the wall.

But we came here for the view, and on a clear day you can really feel that you are standing on the edge of the world, just as those Roman soldiers must have done. Looking back the way we have come, the wall weaves easily over the crags, with the loughs of Broomlee, Greenlee, Crag Lough and Grindon nestling at its feet. Looking west, the highest point of the wall, at Winshields 375m (1,230ft) beckons. Northwards, where the sentries' anxious gaze was directed, the Simonside Hills are backed by the Cheviots and the dim outline of the Southern Uplands of Scotland. To the south above heather-clad Barcombe, Cross Fell and Cold Fell, the highest points of the Pennines, rise on the horizon, and the northern Lakeland fells of Skiddaw and Blencathra are also sometimes just visible.

No one knows what battles were fought defending this last outpost of the Roman Empire, but we do know that it was successfully attacked at least three times before it was finally abandoned at the end of the fourth century.

From Housesteads, the wall rollercoasts over Cuddy's and Hotbank Crags, where there are stunning views of the lakes of Broomlee, Greenlee and Crag Lough. The fort of Vindolanda lies due south at Chesterholm and includes a museum and a full-size reconstruction of a wall section and turret.

Over Steel Rigg and Winshields (the highest point of the wall), the wall drops down to Caw Gap, which is guarded by the fort of Great Chesters (Aescia). Here the well-preserved wall is joined by the Pennine Way as it sweeps along over Walltown Crags and over the broken crags of the Nine Nicks of Thirlwall. Crossing the Tipalt Valley, the wall heads for the River Irthing and Birdoswald fort (Banna), which protected the crossing. There are wonderful panoramic views over the well-wooded meanders of the Irthing Valley from the southern edge of the fort. Lord Carlisle compared the view to that from Troy, and it is indisputably one of the most beautiful views along the route.

Views of the distant Lakeland hills of Blencathra and Skiddaw open up to the left from Coome Crag, but the wall marches inexorably on past the remains of the Pike Hill Signal Tower on Northrigg Hill (where there are more fine views) and on across the lowlands to Carlisle

(Luguvalium), where the Tullie House Museum contains some of the best finds from the western section of the wall.

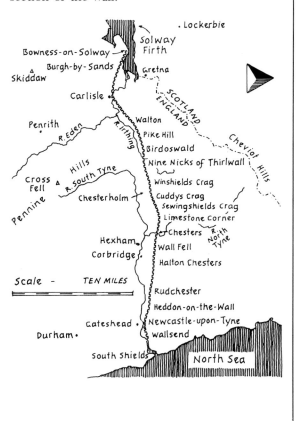

### THE GLENFINNAN MONUMENT

One of the most romantic and enduring stories of an invasion which was in itself a folly, concerns Bonnie Prince Charlie and the 'Glorious '45'. So many myths and legends have grown around the unsuccessful attempt by Prince Charles Edward Stuart to capture the English throne that it is difficult to uncover the truth. What we do know is that this charismatic figurehead of the Jacobean cause landed at Loch nan Uamh, near Arisaig, on 25 July 1745 with a mere seven followers. They marched 12 miles (19km) east through the wild Bounds of Moidart to the head of Loch Shiel where Glenfinnan winds up into the Highlands. And it was here, on 19 August, that Bonnie Prince Charlie raised the red and white silk standard of his father to start his fateful campaign.

The place is marked today by a monument topped by a kilted Highlander, which was built in 1815 at the height of Jacobean romanticism by Alexander MacDonald of Glenaladale. This famous viewpoint on the Road to the Isles carries accounts in Gaelic, Latin and English of Prince Charlie's 'daring and romantic attempt to recover a throne lost by the imprudence of his ancestors'. Bonnie Prince Charlie's attempt to reclaim the crown ended only twelve months later in the ignominy of bloody defeat at the hands of the 'Butcher' Duke of Cumberland at Culloden. The brief rebellion also signalled the end of the Scottish clan system and the start of the infamous Highland clearances. Bonnie Prince Charlie, who probably never knew a word of Gaelic, ended his days as a drunken reprobate in Rome.

*The kilted, romantic statue of a Highlander which stands on top of the Glenfinnan Monument. The pillar and statue, a landmark on the Road to the Isles, was erected in 1815 by Alexander MacDonald of Glenaladale and it became 'the monument of its amiable and accomplished founder' when he died in the same year. Wooded St Finnan's Isle, seen in the loch to the left, had been the burial ground of his clansmen for centuries*

It therefore seems appropriate that the Glenfinnan Monument should feature an ordinary Highlander. It was his traditional way of life that was irretrievably destroyed when the proud but disorderly Scottish rabble marched as far south as Derby, sending panic waves through the kingdom before meeting inevitable and bitter defeat in less than an hour in the appalling carnage on bleak Drumossie Moor, Culloden 1746.

The best view of the Glenfinnan Monument, which marks one of the most famous lost causes in British history, is probably from the roadside itself, where it is framed by the surrounding hills that look on down the glen. Alternatively, to fully appreciate its wild Highland setting, you can climb up the shoulder of Streap from Glen Finnan.

## MORE EYEFUL TOWERS

Britain is so well blessed with monuments and follies that it may seem that every hill and high point has been used for this purpose at one time or another. Some of our favourite follies have been described in this chapter, but many more have had to be omitted. So in an effort to give a more comprehensive coverage of these 'eyeful towers', a few more well-known examples are described here.

One of the most prolific folly builders was Mad Jack Fuller, owner of Brightling Park in Sussex. His 12m (40ft) high Sugar Loaf at Woods Corner, Dallington, was built to fulfil a bet that he could see the spire of Dallington church from his home. He also built many other obelisks and pagodas, including the Brightling Needle, 200m (650ft) up on Brightling Down, from where views extend across the beech-clad valley of the Rother and south to the coast.

Hull's Tower, on the popular viewpoint of Leith Hill in Surrey, crowns the highest point in south-east England, and was built by Richard Hull to exceed the magic 1,000ft (305m) mark above sea level. Thirteen counties are said to be visible from the top. The ugly Hardy Monument on Blackdown Hill, near Abbotsbury in Dorset, looks more like an industrial chimney than a memorial, but the views from it are breath-taking. Because it is in the heart of Thomas Hardy country, many people mistakenly believe that it celebrates the author, but in fact it was erected in 1846 to commemorate Admiral Thomas Masterman Hardy, the hero of Trafalgar, who was, incidentally, a distant relative of the author.

Solomon's Temple on Grin Low near Buxton in the Peak District was erected in 1896 by a local farmer, Solomon Mycock, to provide work for the unemployed. This hollow battlemented tower is now part of a country park and gives extensive views across the lovely Georgian spa town of Buxton with the moors beyond, and to the despoiled landscape created by limestone quarrying to the south.

Chesterton Windmill near Warwick, is another tower of classical design, reputedly the work of Inigo Jones, and was built as an observatory for Sir Edward Peyto in 1632 and later converted to a windmill. It overlooks the earthworks of a late fourth-century Roman fort which is bisected by the Fosse Way, and is a superb viewpoint across the barley belt of Warwickshire's Feldon.

On the summit of Craig-y-Dinas, on Anglesey, in North Wales, stands the famous Anglesey Monument, erected in 1816 to commemorate the victories of Waterloo and the Peninsular War. The bronze hussar on top represents the 1st Marquis of Anglesey and it was raised to the top to the accompaniment of 'a thousand rejoicing voices' forty-four years after the column was built.

The Scottish baronial-style Wallace Monument on Abbey Craig, Causewayhead, just outside Stirling, commemorates another national hero, Sir William Wallace, an obdurate opponent of Edward I's Scottish aspirations. From its clustering turrets and pinnacles can be seen seven battlefields (notably Bannockburn), as well as Arthur's Seat in Edinburgh, the towers of the two Forth Bridges, and the Pentland Hills to the south.

The slim needle of the Glenfinnan Monument, looking
south-west from the slopes of Glen Finnan down Loch
Shiel, with the Beinn Odhar massif rising on the right.

## THE WESTBURY WHITE HORSE

A landmark which legend states was first constructed in celebration of a famous victory against the foreign forces which tried to invade Britain was the original white horse on Bratton Down, near Westbury in Wiltshire. Although the present horse dates only from 1778, it is believed to have replaced a much earlier and cruder creation which local tradition states was cut in celebration of King Alfred's victory over the Danes at the Battle of Ethandun, exactly nine hundred years before.

Ethandun (the name means 'waste down') is thought to have been the nearby village of Edington where the priory church may occupy the position of the defeated Danish king, Guthrum. Alfred's troops rushed down from the plateau above and, according to a contemporary account, 'he attacked the whole pagan army fighting ferociously in dense order, and by divine

*Westbury's classic White Horse, seen here looking north-east, is a landmark on the West Country rail route from Paddington. Above and beyond the horse are the earthworks of Bratton Castle hillfort*

will eventually won the victory, made great slaughter among them, and pursued them to their fortress (Chippenham)'. The battle saw the end of Danish rule in Wessex, and three weeks later, Guthrum was baptised as a Christian, with Alfred serving as his godfather.

What part the extensive earthworks of the Iron Age hillfort of Bratton Castle, on the downs above the present white horse, played in this decisive battle is not known. However, its strategic position may have given Alfred an advantage over the Danes who were camped in the valley below. A strong local tradition supports this view.

Whether Alfred ordered the cutting of the first white horse at Westbury in celebration of his momentous victory over the Danes will probably never be proved, but surviving illustrations of it certainly show a primitive, crescent-tailed animal, which has been described as resembling a 'saddled dachshund'. The present well-proportioned animal was cut by the appropriately named Mr Gee, steward to Lord Abingdon, in 1778, apparently because he objected to the grotesque creature which previously existed there. The white horse is a landmark for miles around, dominating the prosperous dairy-farming country of the Vale of Pewsey, and a prominent feature for

# VIEWS FROM THE BATTLEFIELDS

Although many of our British battlefields are not afforded the same degree of interpretation and prominence as those in other countries, a number of monuments do exist to commemorate them. And as hills have played an important role in many of the most momentous battles which have taken place on British soil, many of those monuments are sited on good viewpoints.

Ethandun, the site of a battle between King Alfred and the Danes in AD878, provides an excellent viewpoint which is marked by the Westbury White Horse at Bratton in Wiltshire. Perhaps the most important battle in early English history was at Hastings, on the date that even modern history students recall. Harold raised his standards of the Dragon of Wessex and the Fighting Man on the ridge top of Senlac, which is now marked by the ruins of Battle Abbey in Sussex; a memorial stone marks the place where he supposedly fell. About a mile away to the south-east lies Telham Hill, from where William's army approached. It provides a good view of Harold's position as the approaching Normans would have seen it.

Scotland does rather better than England in battlefield interpretation, mainly thanks to the work of the National Trust for Scotland. Bannockburn (1314), on the plains below Stirling Castle's crag, is a good example, as is Culloden (1746), near Inverness. But as both sites are in the lowlands the views are not spectacular, despite the excellent explanations and battlefield trails.

The best English battlefield trail, which affords many excellent views across the Leicestershire countryside, is Bosworth Field, where the Plantagenet dynasty gave way to the Tudors in 1485. Ambion Hill, which rises significantly above the arable plains, was Richard III's Yorkist stronghold at the start of the battle, and red-brick Ambion Farm has been converted into an excellent interpretive centre by Leicestershire County Council. Banners usually mark the main positions in the battle.

Nearby, the Civil War battlefield of Naseby is celebrated by a ball-topped obelisk, said to mark the position of the charge of Fairfax's New Model Army, but actually about a mile from the scene of the action. It is a good battlefield to visit because it has changed so little since 1645, and clear views can be obtained of the rolling Northamptonshire countryside from the straight Naseby–Sibbertoft minor road which crosses the battlefield. Unfortunately, this site is now threatened by a motorway extension.

The Battle of Roundway Down (1643), just north of Devizes in Wiltshire, saw perhaps the most decisive victory for the Royalists during the Civil War. Unmarked by any monument, it can easily be appreciated by field paths from Heddington, near Calne, to the strategically placed King's Play Hill. The battle took place on the broad downland fields between Beacon Hill and Roundway Hill. The site of the first, indecisive, battle of the Civil War at Edgehill (1642), is best appreciated from Sanderson Miller's Gothic folly on Edge Hill itself, or from the beacon on the Dassett Hills.

passengers on the Reading–Exeter railway line. From the downs above the white horse, the view commands what the eighteenth-century topographer Gough described as a 'most beautiful prospect'. The horse itself faces west, with distant views of the Mendip Hills to the south-west, across the linen-like folds of the green downs. The view of the neat, trim Enclosure Act landscape of the Vale of Pewsey towards Trowbridge is marred by the unsightly intrusion of the Westbury cement works and its tall smoke-plumed chimney which dominates the immediate foreground.

On a clear day, the view from the heights of the hillfort above the white horse extends north-east to the prehistoric metropolis of Avebury, some 20 miles (32km) away. Other white horses can be spotted from this superb viewpoint: if the conditions are anything like favourable, looking north-east you should be able to pick out at least two with the naked eye, one at Pewsey and the other Alton Barnes, and, with the aid of binoculars, others may be seen.

ABOVE

*High on the rolling Wiltshire downs north of Devizes is the now-peaceful battlefield of Roundway Down, scene of one of the most decisive battles of the Civil War on 13 July 1643. This view is to the south across the battlefield from below King's Play Hill towards Roundway Hill, on the left skyline*

RIGHT

*Newly sheared sheep dot the green pastures of Warwickshire's Dassett Hills, with Edward Belknap's ironstone Beacon prominent on Beacon Hill, overlooking the Vale of the Red Horse. Before Belknap's forced depopulation of the village of Burton Dassett, this scene would have been of a busy village of wattle-and-daub cottages, with a windmill where the Beacon now stands*

### THE DASSETT HILLS

Only one of Britain's extraordinary collection of hill figures was not white for, as already explained, the leucippotomists always favoured the dazzlingly white chalk country of the downs. The unique exception was the now vanished Red Horse of Tysoe which was carved on a hillside where the broad acres of Warwickshire's Feldon rear up to meet the first of the Cotswolds.

Just across the valley, which is still known as the Vale of the Red Horse, lies the delightful little miniature mountain range of the Dassett Hills, now a Warwickshire County Council country park. And standing proudly overlooking the vale and the adjacent wooded escarpment of Edgehill is Edward Belknap's circular beacon tower which

*The honey-coloured ironstone church of All Saints at Burton Dassett carries the nickname of the Cathedral on the Hills, and is actually built into the side of the hill. It is also one of Warwickshire's most attractive and interesting parish churches*

dates from the late fourteenth century. Only sheep and kite-flying children occupy the green formerly quarried 'hills and holes' topography of the Dassett Hills today, but in the fourteenth century, the thriving market town of Burton Dassett paid taxes equal to a quarter of those paid by the prosperous city of Coventry a few miles further north.

Squire Edward Belknap was only interested in making money for himself from the Dassett Hills. The wool trade was booming and English wool was clothing much of Europe. The hills were ideal for rearing sheep. So, by a cold-hearted and deliberate act of depopulation, Belknap turned out a dozen tenant farmers and their families and enclosed 240ha (600 acres) of the hilltop town to make way for the more profitable sheep. There had probably already been some depopulation of the town as a result of the Black Death, but Belknap completed the process by his callous act of depopulation, and Burton Dassett, a market town since Saxon days, joined Warwickshire's long list of deserted medieval villages.

Today's visitors can still find hints of the former importance of Burton Dassett. The delightful warm-brown ironstone church of All Saints is known as the Cathedral in the Hills, and has some fine recently uncovered wall-paintings, and vigorous, humorous carvings around the capitals of the pillars in the north aisle.

The views from Belknap's battlemented beacon, which may have started life as a windmill tower (another wooden post windmill stood on the lower ground near it in 1655), are breathtaking. Looking north, Coventry's famous three spires are visible, and 30 miles (48km) away, the nest of radio masts at Rugby can be seen. The towers of Warwick Castle are 11 miles (18km) away up the broad valley of the Avon, but the immediate foreground is marred by the ominous roofs of the Central Army Ordnance Depot at Kineton and the livid red scar of the new M40 motorway. In the background the dim blue outlines of Shropshire's Clee Hills, 50 miles (80km) away, can sometimes be seen, and, looking west, the sinuous line of the Malvern Hills overlooks Bredon Hill.

Local legend says that in 1642, Oliver Cromwell watched the bloody but inconclusive first battle of the Civil War at Edgehill, which took place on the fields beneath Beacon Hill, from the beacon tower. The truth is that the future Lord Protector was more probably closely involved himself in the bitter fighting that took place between Charles I and the Earl of Essex, said to be re-enacted by ghostly armies in the skies every anniversary of the battle on the evening of 23 October. It is ironic that the actual site of the battle is still under the control of the army and is not accessible to the public.

There are two apocryphal stories of the Battle of Edgehill. The first concerns Sir Jacob Astley, who was by the king's side when he addressed his troops from the summit of Edgehill. Astley was said to have prayed: 'O Lord, Thou knowest how busy I must be this day: if I forget Thee do not Thou forget me!' Also by the king's side was William Harvey, tutor to the royal children, the Prince of Wales and the Duke of York, and later to achieve fame as the discoverer of the circulation of the blood. Harvey took the two future kings to shelter behind a hedge on the edge of the battlefield, believing that they were at a safe distance from the fighting, and began to read to them from a book. 'But he had not read very long before a bullet of a great gun grazed the ground near him, which made him remove his station.' What effect this incident had on Harvey's blood pressure is not recorded, but it is interesting to speculate how history might have been changed if the bullet had struck either of his young pupils.

The Battle of Edgehill is commemorated by another folly, Sanderson Miller's sham Gothic prospect tower known as Radway Castle, built on the summit of Edgehill on the spot where Charles, 'King and Martyr', raised his standard before the fateful battle.

## BROADWAY TOWER

Not far away on the opposite, western slopes of the Cotswolds, stands another classic folly that also enjoys a superb view, in this case, it is claimed, across twelve counties. The Earl of Coventry's Broadway Tower has been described as an 'architectural toy of the Gothic revival'. It stands, hexagonal, battlemented and supported by three circular towers on top of 316m (1,048ft) Broadway Hill, with the twee, much-photographed village of Broadway at its feet.

The story is that the earl built the tower in 1798 to show off to his wife the extent of his land-holdings – to be truly a monarch of all he surveyed. Broadway Tower and the land around it is a country park, so don't expect to pretend to be the Countess of Coventry and have the spectacular view to yourself if you visit the place on a summer Sunday. The tower has a permanent exhibition on the work of William Morris, while outside the park has nature trails and playgrounds for children.

The view from the machicolated top of Broadway Tower extends over much of middle England and as far as the Welsh hills to the west. The chequerboard landscape of the fruitful Vale of Evesham forms the foreground, in which every village could be the model for The Archers' Ambridge and every half-timbered pub seems to be full of Walter Gabriels. A good way to approach the tower is from the beautiful little

# THE COTSWOLD WAY

The Cotswold Way is an unofficial 100 mile (161km) long-distance walk which follows the western scarp of the Cotswold Hills from Bath to Chipping Campden. The brainchild of the Gloucestershire branch of the Ramblers' Association, it provides an almost continuous panorama across the broad Severn Vale to the hills and mountains of Wales beyond.

As might be expected, there are many fine viewpoints from this route, which was designed with fine views in mind, and we visit just one in this chapter at Broadway Tower. Some of the others include the view of the elegant, honey-coloured-stone Georgian city of Bath from Penn Hill, as you leave the Avon valley near the aptly named Prospect Stile. Littledown hillfort is the first of a dozen such structures that you will encounter on the route, and the first of a series of monuments is that to Sir Bevil Grenville who was killed in the Battle of Lansdown during the Civil War. Climbing the scarp to Hawkesbury Upton, you pass the Somerset Monument, and as you enter Gloucestershire, the Way skirts the

Brackenbury Ditches hillfort to reach the rocket-shaped Tyndale Monument, which celebrates William Tyndale who first translated the Bible into English.

From the breezy heights of Stinchcombe Hill, you pass the mysterious tree-topped shape of Cam Long Down, said to have been created when the Devil emptied his wheelbarrow there, to Uley Bury hillfort. Frocester Hill and Coaley Peak give stunning views across the Severn Valley.

From Stroud, the Way rises again to Haresfield and Painswick Beacons, then passes through cool beech woodland to Cooper's Hill. You are now reaching perhaps the most spectacular part of the Way, and the great spur of Cooper's Hill is the scene of the annual Whitsuntide cheese-rolling races. From the maypole, the view extends from May Hill to the left, backed by the Welsh Black Mountains, to the Malverns and Cleeve Cloud above Cheltenham to the north.

Witcombe Woods take the path to the famous viewpoint of Birdlip, and the Crickley Hill Country Park with its important hillfort, which was occupied from the Stone Age through to Roman times.

Leckhampton Hill, above Cheltenham, is famous for the quarried obelisk of the Devil's Chimney (see pp. 60 and 140), while the highest and wildest part of the Way awaits on Cleeve Common, with a summit at 330m (1,083ft) and superb views across Regency Cheltenham and the Vale of Gloucester.

On the last stretch of the walk, you pass perhaps its most important prehistoric monument at the impressive neolithic long barrow of Belas Knap, before you drop down to Winchcombe. The last top is Broadway with its tower, before you descend on the final sweep of the wolds into picturesque Chipping Campden.

original Norman parish church of St Eadburgha which is situated on the Snowshill road out of Broadway. From this plain, simple building, with its unusual central tower and bell-ringing well, paths lead up through the fields to the stark, medieval-looking tower high on the hill above. An alternative approach could be made from Snowshill, with its lovely manor house which is full of 'collector's items' gathered by its former owner, the eccentric Charles Wade. Or you could simply follow the Cotswold Way signs from tourist-choked Broadway, a golden-stone village described by the eminent architectural historian Sir Nikolaus Pevsner as 'the showpiece of England'.

ABOVE _____

*Standing four-square on top of 316m (1,048ft) Broadway Hill on the northern escarpment of the Cotswolds is the Earl of Coventry's Gothic-style Broadway Tower. This prospect tower is now the centre of a country park, but was allegedly built by the earl to impress his lady and show her the extent of his estates*

OVERLEAF _____

*The view looking west from the base of Broadway Tower. The Vale of Evesham stretches below to the right with Bredon Hill 293m (961ft) in the left distance and the dim shape of the Malvern Hills ridge beyond. The sunlit village in the centre on the extreme right is Broadway itself*

ABOVE ————————————————

*The strange obelisk known as the Devil's Chimney on Leckhampton Hill, overlooking Cheltenham on the Cotswold Way, looks natural. In fact, it was created by quarrymen who perversely left the oolitic limestone pinnacle behind as they excavated the stone which helped build the spa town in the valley below*

RIGHT ————————————————

*A view of the cubist blocks of the City of London over the trees of Greenwich Park. One of the twin domes of Sir Christopher Wren's Royal Naval College dominates the middle distance. Historic Greenwich Park is a popular playground for Eastenders, who cross the river by ferry or by Brunel's foot tunnel beneath the Thames. It is also the venue for the start of the London Marathon*

## GREENWICH PARK

More architectural showpieces are to be seen from our next viewpoint, described as having the most breathtaking vista of 'the Great Wen' – London. Greenwich Park is also the oldest of the royal parks, enclosed by the licence of Henry VI in 1433. According to the historian Sir Arthur Bryant, nowhere in England is richer in history and noble architecture than Greenwich. It stands on a green plateau overlooking the great meander of the Thames around the Isle of Dogs and across much of the capital, with the 'pepper-pot' dome of Christopher Wren's St Paul's Cathedral surrounded by the modern towers of the city. Just across the river, the fashionable modern Dock-lands development around Canary Wharf now fills the foreground, with the cubist block of what will be Britain's tallest building taking shape.

Greenwich Park, for television viewers, is that green space just off the bottom-right corner of the picture in the opening titles of *Eastenders* and the place where the London Marathon starts. But for generations, it has also provided a welcome breathing space for the families of East End dockers. Greenwich has also witnessed many of the greatest events in English history, from the triumphant return of Henry V from Agincourt in 1415 to the landing of Charles II from exile at the Restoration in 1660. On the same riverside terrace where Elizabeth I watched Francis Drake's *Golden Hind* return from his circumnavigation of the world, Elizabeth II knighted Sir Francis Chichester for his single-handed voyage nearly four centuries later.

Greenwich was the birthplace of four Tudor monarchs, including Henry VIII and Elizabeth I, and was the favourite home of most of them and their Stuart successors. Here was where Henry VIII courted Anne Boleyn, danced with her under the 'Queen Elizabeth Oak' (which still exists) and where, four months after their marriage, the

*The slightly sinister, black-caped statue of General James Wolfe (1727–59) overlooks the tower blocks and cranes of the Canary Wharf development in London's East End from the highest point of Greenwich Park. Wolfe was the victor of the Battle of Quebec in 1759 when, after being wounded three times, he died in the hour of victory and became a national hero. The chips in the statue's stone plinth were made by shrapnel from wartime bombs – the former docklands were a prime target for the Luftwaffe*

future Good Queen Bess was born. Greenwich Park was traditionally the scene of Sir Walter Raleigh's gallant act of throwing down his cloak so that the queen should not step in a puddle, and here was where the downfall of the Spanish Armada was planned.

But it was Greenwich's classic architecture which brought us here, and the River Thames – called 'liquid history' by one historian – is the finest way to appreciate it and to approach the rolling, tree-lined acres of the park.

Opposite, from the Island Gardens on the Isle of Dogs or from Greenwich Pier, the full Baroque glory of Sir Christopher Wren's masterpiece of the Royal Naval College, with Inigo Jones' classically proportioned Queen's House as the background centrepiece, are seen to best effect. A novel approach from the Isle of Dogs is to take the Brunel foot-tunnel under the Thames.

Wren wanted a grand central domed building facing the river, but Queen Mary insisted on a clear view of the river from the Queen's House where she had been brought up. So Wren was forced to compromise and he designed the twin-domed buildings we see today. These elegant colonnades and porticoes stand on the site of the famous Palace of Placentia, which was the Greenwich Henry and Elizabeth knew, but which was demolished by Charles II. It is a steep walk up behind the Queen's House to the summit of the park, and the Old Royal Observatory. This dates from 1675 and was also designed by Wren 'for the Observator's habitation and a little Pompe', as he honestly put it. That first 'observator' or Astronomer Royal, was the Rev John Flamsteed, and his house stands across the courtyard.

Millions of visitors have stood in the observatory's courtyard and been photographed with one foot in the eastern and one foot in the western hemisphere across the famous Greenwich Prime Meridian, which is marked by a brass line set in the cobbles. Just inside the eastern hemisphere stands the rather sinister, black-caped monument to General James Wolfe, victor at Quebec in 1759, who lived at Macartney House on the edge of the park and is buried in Nicholas Hawksmoor's beautiful parish church of St Alphege in Greenwich village. The view from Wolfe's monument is probably the finest in the park, with both the college and most of London spread out before you, and the low hills of Essex on the other side of the Thames basin beyond. But time spent exploring the rest of the 80ha (200 acre) park, with its avenues of twisted, gnarled Spanish chestnuts and so many echoes of history will be richly rewarded.

'Is this not very fine?' asked Dr Johnson of Greenwich in 1673. 'Yes,' replied the cynical Boswell, 'but not equal to Fleet Street.' If the journalist of today was asked to compare Greenwich Park with the new 'Fleet Street' of 'Fortress Wapping' just upstream across the Thames, there would surely be no contest.

### COOK MONUMENT, EASBY MOOR

Another great hero of the eighteenth century, Captain James Cook, is honoured on a hillside near his home on the north-west edge of the glorious North York Moors. Cook was born at Marton, near Middlesbrough, in 1728, but was to die a hero's death in a lesser-known St Valentine's Day massacre on a far-off Hawaiian shore in 1779. But the circumstances surrounding the placing of the memorial on Easby Moor at 324m (1,064ft)

*A close-up of the Cook Monument, erected in 1829. There was much local controversy about the siting of this monument, for many local people thought it should have been erected on the more prominent landmark of Roseberry Topping (just visible on the skyline to the right)*

Heather moorland on Cold Moor, looking east towards Hasty Bank on the Cleveland Way. The North York Moors National Park has the finest expanse of heather moorland in Britain, and the high moors are ablaze with the purple flowers of this tough plant in late summer

## MANAGING THE MOORLANDS

For most visitors, the fine sweeps of purple heather which clothe upland areas such as the North York Moors are the epitome of a natural, wild landscape, untouched by man. In fact, nothing could be further from the truth. Very few British landscapes are completely natural wildernesses, and our upland moors are no exception. Those rolling acres of royal-hued heather are just as unnatural, in their way, as the regimented battalions of coniferous forestry or the prairies of East Anglia. All these landscapes are skilfully managed by their owners for a crop, whether it be pit props, barley, or, in the case of the moors, red grouse.

The natural, or climax, vegetation of most of Britain would be deciduous woodland, but the ancient natural woodlands of Britain are now very few and far between. Only in places like haunted Wistman's Wood on Dartmoor, or in some rocky cloughs in the Pennines, will you find true natural woodland. On the moors, the trees have been burned or grazed out of existence long ago in a process that was started by Stone Age man. Climatic changes have also affected the trees' chances of regeneration, but today, the moors are managed almost entirely for the benefit of one bird, the plump, furry-footed red grouse (*Lagopus lagopus*). Grouse prefer heather of mixed age for their life-style. They need older, more woody heather for shelter and nesting, but younger shoots for feeding. That fact accounts for the patchwork-quilt appearance of a well-managed moor. The moors are regularly burned, or 'swaled', in the spring to achieve this mixed-age heather. Moorland areas in places like the Peak District are often closed for walking in the weeks following the 'Glorious Twelfth' of August, when the grouse-shooting season begins.

Nowadays, farmers and landowners can earn as much or more from grouse shooting on their moors as they can from raising sheep on them. It is not surprising, therefore, that the grouse is protected so jealously by moorland gamekeepers, or that we have such wonderful displays of heather on our moors in the late summer.

*The views from the squat little obelisk of the Cook Monument are outstanding, extending over green Vale of York, and northwards to shapely Roseberry Topping, 'the Matterhorn of Cleveland'*

were anything but heroic. Heated local argument surrounded the original proposals to place the monument on the top of the prominent conical hill of Roseberry Topping, just north of Airy Holme Farm where Cook spent part of his childhood. Eventually, the substantial iron-railed obelisk was constructed fifty years after his death on the less controversial summit of Easby Moor, 2 miles (3km) to the south.

The blunt, ugly column of local sandstone would not have complemented the graceful lines of Roseberry Topping, which is sometimes called 'Cleveland's Matterhorn'. However, it does impart a certain welcome distinction to the conifer-clad slopes of Easby Moor. Note the quaint old phonetic spelling of Hawaii – 'Owyhee' – in the inscription on the plaque on the monument.

If you approach Easby Moor from the village of Great Ayton, you will eventually meet the way-marked Cleveland Way long-distance path. Leaving the dense conifer plantations of Little Ayton Moor, the path emerges into a sea of heather, which is a joy to walk on in late summer when the flowers are in bloom. Looking east, you will see vast acres of this royal-hued flower – one of the great glories of the North York Moors National Park.

The view from the monument is stunning. Due north, the bracken-covered slopes of Rose-berry Topping lead up to the sheer cliffs of its western face, which were caused not by nature but by undermining by nineteenth-century iron miners. From this angle, the hill looks like a miniature Rock of Gibraltar, and in the middle distance, the white-painted row of miners' cottages at Gribdale Terrace look slightly incongruous.

Roseberry's cliffs frown down over the distant gleaming smokestacks and storage tanks of Teesside's chemical industry, a mere 10 miles (16km) away. At night, the stark profile of Roseberry Topping is thrown into dramatic silhouette by the unearthly orange glow of

Teesside, and the street lights of Middlesbrough sparkle like a field of stars at its feet.

Looking south across Kildale, the flat, incised tableland of the Cleveland escarpment from Cringle Moor to Rosedale Head is revealed, while the fertile Vale of York and the distant Pennines around Stainmore fill the western horizon.

### THE PENSHAW MONUMENT

Further north up the A1 stands one of the strangest monuments in Britain, a blackened northern Parthenon, which imitates the classical Greek Temple of Theseus in Athens. The Penshaw Monument, near Washington in County Durham, was built in 1844 in memory of John George Lambton, the 1st Earl of Durham and former Governor General of Canada, whose family seat was at Lambton Park in the valley of the Wear below. Lord Durham was known as 'Radical Jack' because in 1830 as Lord Privy Seal, he was one of the four compilers of the long-awaited Reform Bill, which abolished the rotten parliamentary boroughs. His time as Governor General of the Province of Canada was equally momentous, and it was his constitution, prepared after his resignation (caused by constant personal criticism), which forms the basis of the dominion's modern laws.

The extraordinary 21m (70ft) high roofless Doric temple on Penshaw Hill is a worthy reminder of the great reformer, whose local nickname was 'King Jog'. It was erected by public subscription – an indication of his popularity – and designed by John and Benjamin Green of Newcastle. It is a landmark for miles around, a strangely surrealistic sight in this former industrial landscape, towering above the River Wear and its former colliery villages of Fatfield, Philadelphia and Shiney Row.

*The extraordinary Doric temple of the Penshaw Monument commands extensive views over the valley of the River Wear. A landmark for miles around, it is a popular weekend picnic place for the people of Durham and the surrounding former coal-mining villages.*

# A ROUTE TO PENSHAW HILL

This easy walk to one of the North East's most famous landmarks can be combined with a visit to an interesting museum and a Wildfowl Trust Reserve. It starts in the unpromising surroundings of Barnes Park, on the edge of industrial Sunderland, where the Grindon Museum contains period rooms and shops on a smaller scale than the more famous Beamish Open Air Museum nearby.

Take the footpath through the park which leads to the left of Grindon Hill, following the valley of the Barnes Burn to Hastings Hill, site of recent archaeological excavations. Follow the footpath to Hastings Hill Farm, where there is a tumulus on the right, to Foxcover Road. Turn right here to cross the busy A19 and then left to branch right again to a plantation. Follow a lane towards Flinton Hill Farm, turning left by the farm to reach the A183.

Penshaw Monument, on its hill ahead, has been prominent for some time, and now you cross the road to ascend the slopes to reach it by the recently constructed wooden steps. After admiring the view, head left down along the edge of the wood towards Penshaw church. In Hill Lane, turn right and follow the field path down the hill, crossing Cox Green Road where there is a sign 'To the Wear'. Turn right by the fine ten-arched Victoria Railway Viaduct, 39m (128ft) above the river, which was opened on the day of Queen Victoria's coronation in 1837. Now take the woodland path right by the river past some ancient staithes to Cox Green and the Washington Wildfowl Trust Park. Set up by the late Sir Peter Scott in 1946, this 40ha (100 acre) park is home to over 1,000 swans, ducks and geese of nearly 200 different species. During the summer, you can catch a pleasure boat back to Sunderland from here.

Follow the riverside path to the impressive limestone cliff of Claxheugh Rock and the former Penshaw–Sunderland railway track, which will lead you back to the suburbs of Sunderland.

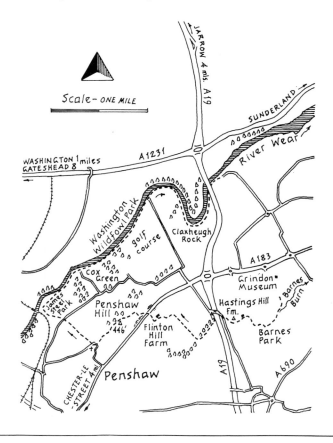

Penshaw, or nearby Worm Hill, is also home to a monster story, linked to one of Radical Jack's forebears who lived at Lambton during the Middle Ages. As a youngster, he caught a strange-looking worm while fishing in the River Wear, and on his way home tossed it into a well by the castle. When he grew up he joined a crusade to the Holy Land, completely forgetting about the worm, which grew to an enormous size and began terrorising the neighbourhood. At night, it would sleep coiled three times around the hill. Attempts to kill it proved fruitless, for each time that it was cut in two, the halves merely joined together again.

When young Lambton returned to England he was horrified at what had happened and con-sulted a local witch to ascertain the best way of disposing of the monster. She advised him to stud his armour with knife blades. This he did and when the Lambton worm coiled itself around him in the ensuing battle, it was literally cut to pieces which were swept away in the River Wear before they could rejoin.

*A view from inside the great, blackened northern Acropolis of the Penshaw Monument. The former mining town of Washington can be seen in the distance through the Doric arches. When the foundation stone of this strange monument to John George Lambton (the first Earl of Durham) was laid in 1844 the ceremony was attended by freemasons from all over the world, led by the Grand Master, the Earl of Zetland*

The Lambton Worm came to life again recently in a sinuous 300m (984ft) work of art by Andy Goldsworthy on the Consett to Sunderland railway, which now incorporates a linear sculpture park.

On my most recent visit to the Penshaw Monument, which is now cared for by the National Trust, there was a veritable procession of people winding up the steps through the flowering hawthorns on the hillside. It is now a popular resort for the people of Tyneside and Wearside and there was a holiday atmosphere about it. The air was filled with the angry buzz

*McCAIG'S FOLLY, OBAN* _____

*The view west from McCaig's Tower, Oban. Ferries plying to and from Mull and the Western Isles glide across the glittering waters of Oban's sheltered harbour, while the hills of Kerrera Island and Mull make up the background*

and snarl of trial bikes, which were raising the dust on the partly reclaimed coal tip opposite Penshaw Hill, sounding like wasps in a bottle. The slightly surrealistic atmosphere was compounded by the vivid yellow fields of oilseed rape in full flower – a 'painting by numbers' landscape – in the fields surrounding the hill. But once you reach the monument, the view is stupendous. The River Wear, graveyard of the legendary worm, winds around the foot of the hill, with the Durham to Newcastle railway line beyond. The tower blocks of Gateshead and Newcastle-upon-Tyne fill the northern skyline, while to the east is Sunderland, birthplace of so much of Britain's former maritime greatness. To the south, the triple towers of Durham Cathedral can just be defined, marking the ancient seat of the Prince Bishops who had ruled this land for so many centuries. But the panoramic view shows a slowly healing landscape, torn apart by the needs of industry and now slowly recovering its sylvan beauty. The collieries have gone and Penshaw is gradually reverting to its ancient name, which means 'wooded hill'.

## McCAIG'S FOLLY, OBAN

Another folly of classical design is a prominent feature and fine viewpoint above the charming Scottish seaside town of Oban, a favourite embarkation point for the Western Isles. McCaig's Folly, or simply 'The Tower', as this mock Colosseum is known, was the creation of John Stuart McCaig, a successful local banker and philanthropist who admired above all the art of Greece and Rome. He saw his Tower as a means of providing employment for local people, a not uncommon *raison d'être* among folly-builders. It was completed in 1890. Approached from Craig-ard Road, Oban's circular Colosseum provides

spectacular views through its pointed, open windows across the Firth of Lorn to Mull, with Ben More prominent, north to Morvern, and inland towards Ben Cruachan.

## MOW COP

A folly which looks down on another industry-scarred landscape is the sham Gothic castle of Mow Cop, which crowns a 335m (1,100ft) much-quarried gritstone summit on the borders of Cheshire and Staffordshire. Built in 1754 by the local squire Randle Wilbraham to adorn the eastern skyline as seen from his home, 3 miles (5km) to the west at Rode Hall, Mow Cop is now in the capable hands of the National Trust. It takes the form of a two-storeyed circular tower alongside a Gothic-arched curtain wall which steps down the hillside. At one time, the tower was roofed and used as a summerhouse, gazebo or prospect tower by Squire Wilbraham and his guests. Mow Cop was also the site of one of Macaulay's chain of Armada beacons, linking Shropshire's Wrekin with Cheshire's Alderley Edge.

Mow Cop's other claim to fame is that it was the birthplace of the Primitive Methodist movement. A simple stone monument beneath the tower records an extraordinary twelve-hour prayer meeting held there on 31 May 1807, organised by a Potteries wheelwright, Hugh Bourne, and his friend William Clowes of Burslem. A century later, over seventy thousand disciples gathered to worship at their 'Holy Mount'.

In one of the worked-out quarries just north of the tower and actually forming the highest point of the hill, stands the isolated leaning gritstone pinnacle known as the Old Man o' Mow. Once the scene of some entertaining rock climbs, the Old Man is now officially out of bounds to the climber. There is evidence of fresh rock falls and a sign bans further exploration. The name is not thought to have been given because of any human resemblance, but may possibly refer to the hill itself, like the Old Man of Coniston in the Lake District or the Old Man of Storr on Skye. My climbing colleague John Cleare cast a critical eye over the Old Man on our last visit, but wisely

*Seen above the masts of the fishing boats tied up on Railway Quay in the West Highland port of Oban, the strange classical Colosseum of McCaig's Folly (or Tower) dominates the view. It was built in 1890 by wealthy banker John Stuart McCaig to provide work for local people*

decided that discretion was the better part of valour. It was a hot summer's day and as we explored the folly and its rocky surrounds, we met a local man who was born within the shadow of the hill. He could well have been the model for the Old Man o' Mow, with his craggy face and thick pebble glasses. He told us that he often visited the hill, admiring the view through his heavy ex-WD binoculars. Weren't his binoculars a little too heavy to hold up for long periods, I wondered? 'I usually use the wife to lean on,' he chauvinistically explained.

Mow Cop is also a popular resort for the people of the Potteries, Congleton and Crewe, and there are outstanding views west over the broad Cheshire plain as far as the Berwyn Mountains of North Wales, north-east to the Peak District and south to the dark conifers of Cannock Chase, with the dim outlines of the

RIGHT

*This extraordinary gritstone rock pinnacle is known as the Old Man of Mow, and it lies in a disused quarry not far from the Mow Cop folly. Like the Devil's Chimney in the Cotswolds, it was left by quarry workers when they excavated the stone all around it, leaving this odd leaning tower for the world to wonder at. Its top forms the highest point of the Mow Cop escarpment, but is seldom visited!*

BELOW

*The dramatic outline of Mow Cop folly, on the edge of the Cheshire hills near Biddulph, is a monument to local squire Randle Wilbraham. Completed in 1754, it commands far-reaching views across the Cheshire Plain to the distant Shropshire and Welsh hills, and the distant Mersey to the west. Mow Cop also lays claim to be a birthplace of the Primitive Methodist movement, and is regarded by followers as their 'Holy Mount'*

Shropshire Hills 50 miles (80km) away. The huge upturned saucer of the Jodrell Bank Radio Telescope is prominent in the plain below, and the tower blocks of Manchester glitter to the north, beyond wooded Alderley Edge.

On the day that we visited Mow Cop, white-rumped house martins swooped in and out of their nests under the battlements of the tower and families were bilberry picking in the heathery slopes below. But the view which attracted our 'Old Man o' Mow' was that looking towards the obviously reclaimed coal tips of Newcastle-under-Lyme and Stoke. 'Look at that!' he exclaimed. 'If someone could paint that, it'd be worth a fortune.' As we left him to his myopic reverie we reflected that beauty, and the views of beauty held by the folly-builders, would always be in the eye of the beholder.

| FACTBOX | | |
|---|---|---|
| | GR | MAP |
| Uffington White Horse, Berkshire | SU303867 | LR174 Newbury & Wantage |
| Housesteads Fort, Northumberland | NY790688 | LR86 Haltwhistle, Bewcastle & Alston |
| Glenfinnan Monument, Loch Shiel | NM906806 | LR40 Mallaig & Loch Shiel |
| Westbury White Horse, Wiltshire | ST898516 | LR184 Salisbury & The Plain |
| Dassett Hills, Warwickshire | SP395520 | LR151 Stratford-upon-Avon |
| Edgehill Tower, Warwickshire | SP37 47 | LR151 Stratford-upon-Avon |
| Broadway Tower, Worcestershire | SP114362 | LR150 Worcester & The Malverns |
| Wolfe's Monument, Greenwich | TQ40 77 | LR177 East London |
| Cook Monument, Easby Moor | NZ582101 | LR93 Middlesbrough & Darlington |
| Penshaw Monument, Durham | NZ32 53 | LR88 Tyneside & Durham |
| McCaig's Folly, Oban | NM86 30 | LR49 Oban & East Mull |
| Mow Cop, Cheshire | SJ855577 | LR118 Stoke-on-Trent & Macclesfield |

# 5
# LITERARY
# LANDSCAPES

Great landscapes and great views inspire great art and literature, and nowhere is this more true than in Britain. Nowhere in the world has the richness and variety of the British landscape, and the British countryside has been the inspiration for some of the world's greatest literature and art.

The Lakeland school of writers and poets, led by William Wordsworth, is often credited with founding the Romantic Movement's interest in natural scenery, but it was another Cumbrian, William Gilpin, who is usually attributed with popularising the picturesque in landscape. Writing some years before Wordsworth in the late eighteenth century, he described the landscape as if it were a painting, stressing that it was the roughness, or 'brokenness', which was the most important ingredient of a picturesque view. Thomas Gainsborough, Peter de Wint and John Constable were among the finest exponents of the picturesque in art.

Yet another category of landscape – the sublime – was promoted by Edmund Burke, writing in 1757. Again anticipating the mood of the Romantic period, Burke defined sublime landscapes as those which overawed the spectator, making him feel insignificant or even threatened. J. M. W. Turner, that supreme artist of light, and James Ward were perhaps the masters of 'sublime' painting, which some people today consider to be overbearing.

## WILLIAM WORDSWORTH: LAKE DISTRICT

It was William Wordsworth's graphic descriptions of the glorious mixture of lakes and mountains in his beloved Lake District, especially around his Grasmere home, which first attracted writers and artists from all over Britain and abroad. Wordsworth was certainly guilty of élitism, preferring to keep his precious Lakeland landscapes for himself and his select band of friends and other 'persons of taste'. He dreaded the influx of 'artisans, labourers and the humbler class of shopkeeper' when he opposed the extension of the railway from Kendal to Windermere in 1844. 'Is then no nook of English ground secure from rash assault?' he thundered in a famous outburst.

However, it was Wordsworth who encouraged, and was directly responsible for, the growth of tourism in the Lake District by the publication in 1810 of his *Guide through the District of the Lakes*. It was in the conclusion of this immediate bestseller that he became the first to suggest that the Lake District should be 'a sort of national property, in which every man has a right and interest who has an eye to perceive and a heart to enjoy'. This often-quoted statement is generally accepted to be the genesis of the National Parks movement.

Wordsworth's élitist attitude to the landscape he loved was shared by many Romantics of the Lakeland school. John Ruskin, who lived at Brantwood on the shores of Coniston Water, complained of 'the certainty of the deterioration of the moral character in the inhabitants of every district penetrated by a railway'. As for the incoming tourists, he imperiously declared: 'I don't want them to see Helvellyn while they are drunk.'

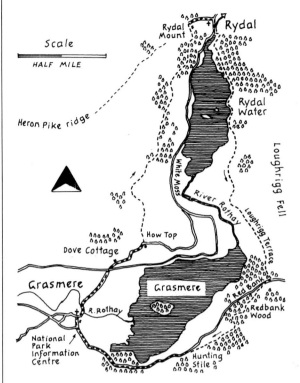

No book covering literary landscapes would be complete without a mention of William Wordsworth's Grasmere, and this easy walk links many of the scenes which inspired the first great populariser of the Lake District. Wordsworth's close relationship with his younger sister Dorothy has attracted much comment, and it is true to say that neither seemed to be truly happy unless one was in the company of the other. Many of Wordsworths' greatest poems were written from Dorothy's minute observations of nature around their home at Dove Cottage at Town End, Grasmere, which for both of them was 'the calmest, fairest spot on earth'.

From this popular National Trust property, turn right and walk up the lane to How Top Farm. Take the track opposite the farm entrance which is signposted to Rydal. This broad stony track leads through the trees under rocky Nab Scar, with the crags of Loughrigg Fell reflected in the still waters of Rydal Water below to the right. Descending into Rydal village with Wansfell glowering ahead, you emerge above Rydal Mount, the Wordsworths' home from 1813 after they outgrew Dove Cottage. Walk down the lane past the church to cross the A591, turning right opposite the Glen Rothay Hotel to cross the River Rothay by the Steps End footbridge. Now follow the river bank right and go through a kissing-gate to enter Rydal Woods.

Passing the old slate quarries, now softened by nature, you emerge on Loughrigg Terrace, one of the Lakeland's finest low-level panoramic walks, which is eminently suitable for a day when the clouds are down on the tops. There are superb views of Grasmere lake ahead, framed by the hills of Helm Crag, Steel Fell, Seat Sandal and Heron Pike. Wordsworth described this view in 'The Excursion':

> The Valley, opening out her bosom, gave
> Fair prospect, intercepted less and less,
> O'er the flat meadows and indented coast
> Of the smooth lake, in compass seen:

Pass through another kissing-gate and keep left between walls through the wood to bear right at a fork and join the minor road. Turn right and enter Red Bank Woods by a track on the left, with lovely views over the lake to Heron Pike. Rejoin the road at Hunting Stile and walk the mile down into Grasmere village, where, beneath the yews in the churchyard of St Oswald, are the simple family graves of William and his wife Mary, with Dorothy, faithful even in death, beside hem. It is a short half mile back to Dove Cottage along the road.

## CAT BELLS

*For the amount of effort required to reach its rocky little summit, Cat Bells repays with as fine a view of lake and mountain as any in the Lake District. Looking north, almost the entire length of Derwentwater is revealed, with the town of Keswick sheltering beneath the smooth slopes of Skiddaw, and Blencathra to the right. The lake glimpsed on the left is Bassenthwaite*

### BEATRIX POTTER: CAT BELLS

No such double standards of upper-middle-class élitism governed the actions of one of the Lakeland's most famous 'in-comers', who did more than many natives towards the conservation of the district. London-born Mrs William Heelis, better known as Beatrix Potter and the creator of Peter Rabbit, was one of the earliest and greatest benefactors of the National Trust, which now owns about a quarter of the Lake District National Park. She bequeathed the heavily visited Tarn Hows near Hawkshead and a number of farms, including her own home at Near Sawrey, to the charity. She was also a noted breeder of the native white-faced Herdwick sheep and did much to ensure the survival of this hardy, ancient and now rare breed.

The inspiration for Beatrix Potter's charming watercolour creations was the farms and fells around her adopted home. The scenes which were the backdrops to her children's fantasies can still be identified today, especially in the craggy tarn-dotted landscape around the Claife Heights and Hill Top Farm, Sawrey, which has now become one of Lakeland's biggest and most congested visitor attractions.

One of my family's favourite Beatrix Potter stories is *The Tale of Mrs Tiggy-Winkle*, but for the setting of that charming tale of the washerwoman hedgehog, we have to go about 20 miles (32km) north to the prominent little conical mountain peak of Cat Bells 451m (1,481ft), which overlooks Derwentwater and Keswick from the south. Here, in the story, 'Lucie climbed upon the stile and looked up at the hill behind Little-town – a hill that goes up – up – up – into the clouds as though it had no top!' Of course, Cat Bells does have a top, and a most satisfying and attainable top with a splendid view too, especially for young legs perhaps setting out on their first Lake District climb.

I will always remember my first visit to that airy, rocky little summit, with its breathtaking views across island-studded Derwentwater to the ridges of Blencathra and north into the mountain-hemmed jaws of Borrowdale. A proud father with his infant son emerged onto the summit from Brandlehow. 'There,' he beamed.

'That's his first real mountain, and I hope it'll be the first of many just like it was for me.'

Cat Bells is that sort of a mountain, a friendly, family fell and the ideal place to introduce young or old to the simple pleasures of fell-wandering. Alfred Wainwright, doyen of generations of Lakeland fell-walkers, describes it as 'one of the great favourites, a family fell where grandmothers and infants can climb the heights together, a place beloved.'

Beatrix Potter certainly seemed to have been in love with Cat Bells. The Lucie in the story was actually Lucie Carr, daughter of the vicar of Newlands, who lived in the vicarage in the hamlet of Little Town below the western slopes of the hill. Lucie scrambled up the steep pathway from the farm of Skelgill, which is still there, virtually unchanged, today. The little wooden door which marked Mrs Tiggy-Winkle's home may well have been a boarded-up shaft of the old Yewthwaite lead-mines, the remains of which can still be seen near the summit.

A more recent visit I made to Cat Bells was a magical one, for an early start from the Gutherscale car park meant that we were on the summit to catch the dawn rising over Derwentwater. The still waters shimmered like a sheet of burnished copper as the great red molten disc of the sun crept up over the shoulders of Blencathra, where I had enjoyed some scrambling the day before. Beneath our feet, the tree-topped islands of Rampsholme, St Herbert's and Derwent Isle were silhouetted against the glittering gold of the lake, and we watched spellbound as the sun slowly chased the velvety shadows from Robinson, Scope End and Hindscarth at the head of the Newlands Valley.

RIGHT _____

*John Ruskin considered the view from Friar's Crag, on the shores of Derwentwater near Keswick, to be one of the finest in Europe, and few of the thousands of visitors who come here annually would disagree. The crag must be the most photographed piece of rock in the Lake District, but the view of the distant Cat Bells reflected in Derwentwater never seems to pale. This was the embarkation point for monks visiting the recluse St Herbert, who lived on wooded Derwent Island – hence the crag's name*

### GEORGE BORROW: SNOWDON

A mountain which has myths and legends inextricably woven into its persona is one we have already visited in Chapter 2. Snowdon, or, more correctly the reigning peak of Yr Wyddfa, is associated with the legends of King Arthur and the Afanc, and, as well as being the highest mountain south of the Border, it also has one of the finest views.

Writing in 1770 about the view from the summit, Craddock claimed: 'It is doubted whether there is another circular prospect so extensive in any part of the terraqueous globe.' But perhaps the most effusive account of the view and the already popular climb to the top of Yr Wyddfa came from the pen of George Borrow, a Norfolk-born linguist and inveterate rambler, in that classic among the early guidebooks, *Wild Wales*, published in 1862. Borrow was an extra-

*The fussy little train of the Snowdon Mountain Railway approaches the summit of Yr Wyddfa, taking those who cannot, or will not, walk to the highest point of Britain outside Scotland. This view looks north-west, down towards Llanberis and the Cwellyn valley to the left*

ordinary character, fascinated by different languages and with an exceptional talent for learning and translating them. Before he was 18, he was said to have mastered no fewer than thirteen different languages, and claimed to have taught himself Welsh by twice reading through a Welsh version of *Paradise Lost*.

Borrow was also an extraordinarily joyful walker who thought nothing of walking 20 or 30 miles (32–48km) a day at an average speed of 'four miles and a half in the hour'. When he came to Wales in 1854 for a walking tour with his wife Mary and teenage stepdaughter Henrietta, his fertile imagination had already been fired by 'the land of old renown and of wonder, the land of Arthur and Merlin'. He was keen to show off his mastery of the Welsh tongue, and unmercifully buttonholed everyone he met along the road, keen to impress them with his apparent fluency in their language.

One of the major objectives of Borrow's tour was the ascent of Snowdon. 'Perhaps in the whole world there is no region more picturesquely beautiful than Snowdon,' he wrote, 'a region of mountains, lakes, cataracts and groves, in which Nature shows herself in her most grand and

beautiful forms.' Borrow and Henrietta set off arm-in-arm from Llanberis, with Borrow 'singing at the stretch of his voice' a Welsh proverb which he freely translated: 'It is easy to say yonder is Snowdon; but not so easy to ascend it.' He advised Henrietta to 'brace up her nerves and sinews' for the attempt, with Mary 'not deeming herself sufficiently strong to encounter the fatigue of the expedition'.

The long and boring Llanberis Path seems to have been as popular in 1854 as it is today, for Borrow noted groups of people and individuals going up or descending the path 'as far as the eye could reach'. Eventually, after a fairly uneventful walk, the couple reached the summit, and Borrow inevitably launched into another of his bombastic monologues. One can imagine Henrietta's embarrassment as her stepfather harangued her:

> Here you are on the top crag of Snowdon, which the Welsh consider, and perhaps with justice, to be the most remarkable crag in the world; which is mentioned in many of their old wild romantic tales, and some of the noblest of their poems . . . You are now on the top crag of

*Snowdon is not to be underestimated by the walker, as this 'Alpine' photograph, taken in March, shows. Ice-coated snow blankets the summit, as walkers make their careful way up the 'tourist track' from Llanberis, following in the footsteps of George Borrow and his daughter. In weather conditions like this it is advisable to take crampons and an ice axe (and know how to use them) if you are venturing off the main paths*

> . Snowdon, generally termed Yr Wyddfa, which means a conspicuous place or tumulus, and which is generally in winter covered with snow; about which snow there are in the Welsh language two curious englynion or stanzas consisting entirely of vowels with the exception of one consonant, namely the letter 'R' . . .

Before long Borrow had lapsed into that strange poem, which soon attracted a crowd of disbelieving tourists. Borrow was delighted when he was mistaken for a Welshman by one of these observers, who turned out to be Welsh himself.

Borrow's description of the view from Yr Wyddfa still takes some beating:

# BORROW'S WILD WALES

George Borrow was an enthusiastic walker and his book entitled *Wild Wales*, in which he describes his four-month perambulation through that country in 1854, remains one of the classics of open-air literature. As well as his ascent of Snowdon, Borrow also visited a number of other Welsh sights and some of his descriptions are worth repeating, if only to admire his boundless enthusiasm for the landscape, which was so different from that of his native Norfolk.

Borrow regularly tramped more than 20 miles (32km) a day, day after day, whatever the weather. He insisted, for example, that he must walk into Wales alone, 'as by walking I would be better able to see the country . . . than by making the journey by the flying vehicle'. So, leaving his wife and daughter to catch the train, he marched the 20 miles (32km) from Chester to Llangollen.

After exploring North Wales and Anglesey, including the ascent of Snowdon, he marched south over the Berwyn moors into mid-Wales. The lovely waterfall at Llanrhaiadr exceeded all the remarkable cataracts in Britain, he believed. 'I never saw water falling so gracefully, so much like thin beautiful threads as here,' he wrote, although he objected to an 'ugly' black rock which 'intercepted' the sight.

Borrow's ascent of Pumlumon (Plynlimon) at 752m (2,467ft), the highest point of mid-Wales, is one of the best passages in his book, as he describes how he drank in turn from the sources of the Rheidol, the Severn and the Wye. He explained to his guide:

It is not only necessary for me to see the sources of the rivers, but to drink of them, in order that in after times I may be able to harangue about them with a tone of confidence and authority.

His description of the view from the summit cairn is one of his best:

A mountainous wilderness extended on every side, a waste of russet-coloured hills, with here and there a black, craggy summit. No signs of life or cultivation were to be discovered, and the eye might search in vain for a grove or even a single tree.

Leaving Llandovery, which he had no hesitation in saying was 'about the pleasantest little town in which I have halted in the course of my wanderings', Borrow heads into the teeth of the 'elemental hurly-burly' of a gale towards the wilderness of the Black Mountains. 'Night was now coming on fast, and, rather to my uneasiness, masses of mist began to pour down the side of the mountain.' Soon even he was obliged to slacken his pace as the mist swept down 'and was so thick that I could only see a few yards in front of me'. Eventually, as he approached the welcome inn at Gutter Vawr after walking for 20 miles (32km) in the soaking mist and rain, he even abandoned his trusty umbrella. 'It was impossible for me to be more drenched than I was,' he explains. All hillwalkers will recognise that final dripping resignation to the elements.

There we stood enjoying a scene inexpressibly grand, comprehending a considerable part of the main land of Wales, the whole of Anglesey, a faint glimpse of part of Cumberland; the Irish Channel, and what might be either a misty creation or the shadowy outline of the hills of Ireland. Peaks and pinnacles and huge moels stood up here and there, about us and below us, partly in glorious light, partly in deep shade.

But it was the llyns or lakes of Snowdon 'which, like sheets of ice or polished silver, lay reflecting the rays of the sun in the deep valleys at our feet' which impressed him most.

In complete contrast to Borrow's effusion but nevertheless among my favourite accounts of the ascent of Snowdon, are the lines from the famous old Locked Book, used by the early climbers at the Pen-y-Gwryd Hotel, on the Capel Curig side of the Llanberis Pass:

> Been up Snowdon,
> A nice ascent.
> William Boden,
> Burton-on-Trent.

## SIR WALTER SCOTT: EILDON HILLS

One of George Borrow's pet prejudices, alongside Roman Catholics, all 'Scotchmen' and, having been born a hated 'Saxon' himself, was the work of Sir Walter Scott, during his day one of the most popular poets and novelists. Writing in *Wild Wales*, he describes Scott's *Woodstock, or the Cavalier* as 'a tiresome, trashy publication', mainly for its 'base fulsome adulation of the worthless great'. Critics may detect a trace of envy in Borrow's statement that this 'trumpery' publication had attracted advance orders amounting to £6,000 from the nation's booksellers. 'They knew the book would please the base, slavish taste of the age, a taste which the author of the work had had no slight share in forming.' Borrow was obviously in the minority, however, because Scott's historical works, almost without exception, were bestsellers.

To find the inspiration which fired this sickly son of an Edinburgh lawyer, we must travel to the Scottish borders, around the prominent triple peaks of the Eildon Hills. Scott's love of the countryside around Melrose stemmed from youthful visits to relatives living in the valley of the River Tweed, where he had been sent when he was suffering from polio. After spending some months with an aunt in Kelso, Scott said that he remembered 'distinctly the awaking of that delightful feeling for the beauties of natural objects which has never since deserted me'. The neighbourhood of Kelso, 'the most beautiful, if not the most romantic, village in Scotland', presented him with objects 'not only grand in themselves, but venerable from their associations'.

Much later, after the publication of two volumes of ballads and *The Lay of the Last Minstrel*, Scott was appointed Sheriff of Selkirkshire, and he rented and later bought a small house at Ashestiel, on the southern bank of the Tweed. It was to be his country retreat for the next eight years, where he wrote *Marmion* and, most successfully, *The Lady of the Lake*, which was a major factor in opening up Loch Katrine and the Trossachs to tourists.

In 1811, Scott bought a small farm called Cartley Hole by the Tweed 3 miles (5km) west of Melrose, within sight of his beloved Eildons. Over the next dozen years, the house was extended at great expense into the vast, many towered mansion of Abbotsford, where Scott fulfilled his ambition to live like a feudal lord. Here, he entertained on the lavish scale of 'the worthless great', which Borrow so despised. With debts mounting, Scott turned to churning out historical novels – fourteen in one six-year period – as he became increasingly fascinated with the medieval times he so much admired. The area around Melrose and the Eildons predictably features strongly in Scott's work. In the poem 'The Eve of St John', he refers to:

> Where fair Tweed flows round holy Melrose,
> And Eildon slopes to the plain

This poem is based on the sixteenth-century romantic ruin of Smailholm Tower, a fine viewpoint on a rocky knoll 7 miles (11km) east of Melrose and a favourite haunt of Scott as a boy

# A Traverse of the Eildon Hills

This route was suggested by my colleague in this book, John Cleare, who describes the Eildons as 'a well-connected *bonne bouche.*'

From the A6091 Melrose–St Boswells road, take the farm track south towards the Eildontree Plantation, which takes its name from a border ballad recounted by Scott in his poem 'The Eve of St John'.

Go left along the plantation edge to find a well-defined path that leads steeply up towards the eastern ridge of Eildon Hill North, which is ringed by the earthworks of the hillfort built by the Selgovae. There are fine views from its 404m (1,325ft) summit. Take the obvious path which leads south-west down to the wide saddle which separates the North from the Mid summits. From here go left on a track and then strike off to the right on a narrow path past the ancient Siller Stane to contour around the south-east slopes of Eildon Wester Hill to the edge of Broad Wood.

Keep left at all junctions until you meet the forestry track which comes up from Greenside Plantation. Follow the track until you reach a vague path which leads steeply up to the small cairn on top of Eildon Wester Hill 371m (1,217ft). A path descends gently north to the wide col and then ascends steeply up scree slopes to the crowning summit of Eildon Mid Hill 422m (1,385ft), where there is a useful toposcope and trig point. Descend the steep path to the northern saddle again, and then drop down south-east to the edge of Old Wood. A wide track just inside the wood leads east above Eildon Hall in the trees below. When you reach a path that comes up from the right from the Hall, follow it left across open moorland eventually to reach your ascent route near a gate. Go right alongside Eildontree Plantation again to rejoin the road.

Scale   —   ONE MILE

when he stayed with his grandfather near Roxburgh. The Cistercian abbey of Melrose, where Robert the Bruce's heart is buried, is another favourite subject.

Almost inevitably, the northernmost summit of the Eildon Hills is crowned by a massive 16ha (39 acre) hillfort dating from the Iron Age, and it has its own familiar legend of King Arthur's sleeping knights. Up to a thousand people of the Selgovae tribe may have lived here at the time of the Roman invasion of Britain. After the Romans captured the site in AD79, they constructed a wooden signal station inside a circular enclosure on the 400m (1,300ft) summit to watch over their camp of Trimontium ('the three hills') 1½ miles (2.4km) to the north-west.

The Eildons stand out as a heather-covered island in a sea of rich lowland farming country south of Melrose in the heart of Scott country.

*Yellow moor grass bends in the wind in this picture looking south-east from the summit of Eildon Hill North. The sunlit village in the centre of the wide Vale of the River Tweed is Newtown St Boswells, and the dark belt of trees is Old Wood, which shelters ancient Eildon Hall. The northernmost Eildon was also the site of an Iron Age hillfort and a Roman signal station*

*This was one of Sir Walter Scott's favourite views of his beloved Eildon Hills – still known as Scott's View – westward from the slopes of Bemersyde Hill. The triple peaks of the Eildons stand above the sweeping oxbow bend of the River Tweed, in delightfully sylvan surroundings near the town of Melrose*

They can be reached in an easy 3 mile (5km) walk from the centre of Melrose, and the views from the northernmost summit are superb in all directions. To the south, the brooding bulk of the Cheviots form the horizon, while northwards, the Moorfoot and Lammermuir Hills dominate the view up Lauderdale. To the west, the rolling, rarely visited hills of Galloway are unhappily marred by unsightly blocks of forestry plantations.

## R. D. BLACKMORE: EXMOOR

An author who used local legends as the substance of his stories was Richard Doddridge Blackmore, who is now chiefly remembered for a single novel. *Lorna Doone – A Romance of Exmoor* was published in 1869 and satisfied the apparently insatiable Victorian taste for thwarted love, blood-thirsty villains, and high, melodramatic passion. The story was based on well-documented tales which Blackmore had heard repeated as a child when he was educated, like John Ridd in the book, at Blundell's School, Tiverton.

Around 1650, a notorious band of outlaws had their stronghold in the then-remote Badgworthy Valley, and legends of the atrocities which they committed were common among Exmoor people. Blackmore even states in one footnote in the book: 'This vile deed was done beyond all doubt.' The fact that he knew and loved the landscape of Exmoor well is obvious from his writing. But, like many authors, he often adapted his descriptions of the scenery to fit his plot. He wrote later:

If I had dreamed that it ever would be more than a book of the moment, the descriptions of scenery – which I know as well as my garden – would have been kept nearer to their fact. I romanced therein, not to mislead any other, but solely for the uses of my story.

Blackmore could never have imagined the huge 'Dooneland' tourist industry which followed the publication of his most successful novel, and which continues even today. Readers avidly retrace the steps of heroine Lorna and her lover John Ridd, making the pilgrimage to the pretty little square-towered church of Oare, where their wedding was tragically ended by the dramatic intervention of the villainous Carver Doone.

For Blackmore, the landscape of Exmoor 'lay softly', but for another author who loved the place, Henry Williamson, Exmoor was

the high country of the winds, which are to the falcons and the hawks; clothed by whortleberry bushes and lichens and ferns and mossed trees in the goyals, which are to the foxes, the badgers, and the red deer; served by rain clouds and drained by rock-littered streams, which are to the otters.

And the most famous of those Exmoor otters was, of course, Williamson's Tarka.

Blackmore's finest description of Exmoor is perhaps Lorna's first impression of the Doone Valley:

For she stood at the head of a deep green valley, carved from the mountains in a perfect oval, with a fence of sheer rock standing round it, eighty feet or a hundred high; from whose brink black wooded hills swept up to the sky-line. By her side a little river glided out from underground with a soft dark babble, unawares of daylight; then growing brighter, lapsed away, and fell into the valley. There, as it ran down the meadow, alders stood on either marge, and grass was blading out upon it, and yellow tufts of rushes gathered, looking at the hurry.

Hoccombe Combe, a tributary of Badgworthy Water between Badgworthy Lees and Badg-worthy Hill south of Malmsmead, is generally believed to be Blackmore's model for the Doone Valley. It is an easy and popular walk up the valley from Malmsmead, past the memorial to Black-more, to reach this secluded, heather-clad valley.

# A Route to the Doone Valley

From Malmsmead, where a farm claims to be Lorna Doone's, follow the signposted narrow lane south to where it bends sharply right. Go straight ahead through a gate along a signposted bridleway. To the left is Badgworthy Water, and Cloud Farm, over the stream, offers refreshments. Walk on past the memorial stone to R. D. Blackmore and pass through another gate. The track now bends around the foot of Great Black Hill which rises above the stunted oak trees to the right. Where the steep valley of Lank Combe comes in from the right, cross the stream by the footbridge. Continue south past Badgworthy Lees to your right, with the heathery slopes of South Common Deer Park to your left.

As you approach Badgworthy Hill, the valley of Hoccombe Combe reveals itself to the right. This is supposedly the model for the Doones' valley, and the few scattered stones which were once cottages on the right are claimed by some to be Carver's home. Climb the steep footpath through the heather across Badgworthy Lees to reach the Withycombe ridge and descend to cross the head of Lank Combe.

At a junction of pathways, take the one signposted to Malmsmead which leads east across the moor towards Malmsmead Hill 388m (1,274ft), a fine viewpoint with prospects extending from Countisbury Head to the west to Porlock Bay to the east. Now you must drop down to a lane, crossing it to a metal gate, from which a bridleway leads down left of Southern Ball Hill. At a division of the track, go left towards Southern Wood, turning right at the road and into the cool of the mossy trees. Passing over a small rise, you soon re-enter Malmsmead. You may wish to stroll through the village the half mile to Oare church, scene of the shooting in *Lorna Doone*, and another 'must' for followers of the Doone Country trail.

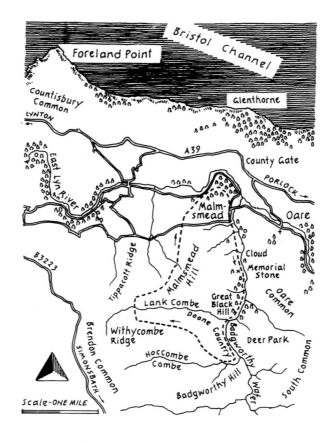

The more energetic might wish to continue up the valley to the heights of Brendon Common and across the Exe plain (where the River Exe starts its circuitous journey to the English Channel) to reach the wind-swept moorland of The Chains – the real roof of Exmoor's 'high country of the winds'. From here, the glittering waters of the Bristol Channel are backed by the first blue hills of Brecon in Wales, while Dartmoor broods dramatically to the south.

## THOMAS HARDY'S WESSEX

Although Blackmore is considered to be one of the finest exponents of the Victorian pastoral novel, he is generally remembered only as a 'one-novel' author, whereas his young friend and contemporary, Thomas Hardy, was much more prolific and successful. Hardy's string of stirring novels set in the soft rich lushness of the Wessex countryside around his home near Dorchester acknowledge him as the master of the genre.

Hardy was born in 1840 in an idyllic thatched-roof cottage at Higher Bockhampton, on the edge of what was then the extensive waste of Egdon Heath, where so many of his dramas were to unfold. But Hardy's Wessex spread much further than his native heaths to cover most of King Alfred's ancient kingdom, from Oxford (Christminster) in the north to Penzance (Pen Zephyr) in the west and Aldershot (Quartershot) in the east. Several of the sites that we have already visited feature in Hardy's novels and poems, including Glastonbury (Glaston in 'A Trampwoman's Tragedy'); Cadbury Castle (Camelot in 'Channel Firing'); and on the Dorset Coast, Ringstead Bay and Lulworth Cove (Ringsworth Shore and Lullstead or Lulwind in 'The Distracted Preacher') and Durdle Door (in 'The Bird-Catcher's Boy'). Hambledon Hill, on which Hardy was apparently once lost in a fog, enters Tess's troubled thoughts during her journey

*Looking north-west from Malmsmead Hill, 388m (1,274ft) north of the Doone Valley. The rounded hill in the distance is Kipscombe Hill which overlooks Countisbury Head and the waters of the Bristol Channel. Old Barrow Hill rises to the right*

home from Flintcombe Ash in *Tess of the D'Urbervilles*.

Viewpoints abound in Hardy's Wessex, which, like Wordsworth's Grasmere and Blackmore's Exmoor, is now firmly implanted in tourist board itineraries. Many consider Hardy's poem 'Wessex Heights' perhaps his greatest, and in it he explains what the high places meant to him:

> There are some heights in Wessex, shaped as if by a kindly hand
> For thinking, dreaming, dying on, and at crises when I stand,
> Say, on Ingpen Beacon eastward, or on Wylls-Neck westwardly,
> I seem where I was before my birth, and after death may be.

Ingpen is Inkpen Beacon, near Newbury, and Wylls-Neck is Wills Neck, the highest point of the Quantocks, at either end of the broad compass of Hardy country.

For a true taste of Hardy's Wessex, you must climb to those heights like Hambledon Hill, with its edge-of-the-world view across Blackmoor Vale, Hardy's Vale of the Little Dairies, to the hill-top town of Shaftesbury (Shaston); or the great multivallate hillfort of Maiden Castle (Mai Dun) on the outskirts of Hardy's later home of Dorchester (Casterbridge). Here, Hardy painted one of his most powerful evocations of place and mood in the short story *A Tryst at an Ancient Earthwork*. Or you should go to remote Eggardon Hill, south-west of Maiden Newton, which is the Haggardon mentioned in *The Trumpet Major* and the 'hill-fortress of Eggar' in the poem 'My

*A winter's evening view of Shaftesbury taken from near the abbey ruins, looking south-west over the tower of the parish church of St James to the distant Vale of Blackmoor. This was country which Thomas Hardy knew well. He called Shaftesbury 'Shaston' and it played a large part in his novel,* Jude the Obscure. *Five miles to the south in Hardy's 'Vale of the Little Dairies' lies Marnhull which became 'Marlott' in* Tess of the d'Urbervilles

Cicely'. Here, on the deeply ridged pastures created by generations of sheep grazing, you will be as close to the heart of Hardy as you are ever likely to get.

## A. E. Housman: Wenlock Edge

Hardy was a Wessex man through and through, and his native landscape exerted a strong influence over all his work. But it is odd that just one book should for ever link A. E. Housman with Shropshire. He was not a son of that county, nor did he live there for any length of time, but this complex academic, who always regarded himself not as a poet but as a professor of Latin first and foremost, is now always associated with that lovely borderland county. This was chiefly through the publication in 1896 of a collection of his poems under the title *A Shropshire Lad*. Published at first under the *nom de plume* of Terence Hearsay, the work became very popular, although for many years Housman stubbornly refused to take any royalties from its sales.

Alfred Edward Housman was born at Fockbury, near Bromsgrove in Worcestershire, and developed his talent for verse at school. He was also a great walker, who loved to ramble on the low hills around his home, casting wistful eyes westwards to the 'blue remembered hills' which were later to earn him so much unwanted fame. From his home, Mount Pisgah, near Bromsgrove, he could see the brooding bulk of the Long Mynd, Wenlock Edge and the sharp beckoning point of The Wrekin, all in neighbouring Shropshire.

Housman's education took him to Oxford, and then he moved to London, but he always yearned nostalgically for those views of the Midland hills which represented the happiest times of his childhood, and perhaps of his life:

> Into my heart an air that kills
> From yon far country blows:
> What are those blue remembered hills
> What spires, what farms are those?

The rich agricultural landscape of south-east Shropshire is dominated by the long wooded Silurian limestone escarpment of Wenlock Edge, featured by Housman in *A Shropshire Lad*. With Ape Dale to the north-west and Corve Dale to the south-east, Wenlock Edge always reminds me of a Peakland 'edge', although it is much more wooded and softer in texture. It is a place abounding in history and tradition, and The Ditches hillfort, now lost in the depths of Mogg Forest, shows that, even in prehistoric times, early man found the commanding views from the Edge to his liking.

About a mile south from The Ditches in remote Hope Dale lies gabled Wilderhope Manor, surely one of the most romantic youth hostels in Britain. Built in 1586, it is a complete and virtually unchanged Tudor manor, and the ancestral home of the Smallman family. One of the early lords of the manor was Major Thomas Smallman, a supporter of the king during the Civil War. Returning home one day to Wilderhope, Major Smallman was captured by a waiting band of Roundheads and imprisoned in an upper room in the house. He escaped by the garderobe (an early lavatory shoot) and grabbed his horse from the stables. Pursued by his captors, the Major made for the nearby scarp of Wenlock Edge, somewhere in the vicinity of the present limestone quarry at Stretton Westwood. Seeing another band of Roundheads approaching from Much Wenlock, he unhesitatingly turned his horse towards the cliff-top and plunged from view. The Roundheads assumed that no one could survive such a fall and turned for home. But, according to the legend, the Major had landed in a crab-apple tree as his horse was dashed to its death at the foot of the crag. The site of the Major's Leap is still marked on the OS map, above Blakeway Coppice on the still wooded scarp of Wenlock.

An earlier legend of Wenlock Edge concerns the robber giant Ippikin who kept his ill-gotten treasure in a cave in the rock. Anyone who finds

Overleaf
*The long wooded scarp face of Wenlock Edge rises steeply to the east above the cornfields near the hamlet of Lushcott in Upper Ape Dale, Shropshire. The dark line of trees marking Easthope Wood could have been in A. E. Housman's mind when he wrote the famous line, 'On Wenlock Edge, the wood's in trouble'*

the cave and recites: 'Ippikin, Ippikin, keep away with your long chin!' will apparently be greeted by the ghost of Ippikin himself. Ippikin's Rock is also marked on the map, near the hamlet of Hilltop.

It must have been a stormy autumn day when Housman described the view from Wenlock Edge in *A Shropshire Lad*:

> On Wenlock Edge, the wood's in trouble;
> His forest fleece the Wrekin heaves;
> The gale, it plies the saplings double,
> And thick on Severn snow the leaves.

The Wrekin is plainly visible to the north from the highest point of the Edge, near Hilltop, while to the west, the higher Shropshire hills of Caer Caradoc and the Long Mynd lie across the green valley of Ape Dale. Immediately below the Edge, the stumpy tower of Hughley church can be seen peeping above the roofs of the village. But the poem clearly states:

> The vane on Hughley's steeple
> Veers bright, a far-known sign,
> And there lie Hughley people,
> And there lie friends of mine.

It was pure poetic licence, explained by Housman because the steeple he had wanted to write about had 'an awkward, ugly name', generally thought to be Tardebigge, near Bromsgrove, where many of Housman's childhood friends from his 'land of lost content' lay buried.

A good, if often muddy, footpath threads the length of the Wenlock Edge woods, which are easily reached by the B4371 from Much Wenlock. The views through the trees across oddly named Ape Dale are very fine and access is free, as most of the land is now thankfully in the hands of the National Trust.

## THE BRONTË SISTERS: HAWORTH MOORS

No such poetic licence was required by the famous and talented Brontë family of Haworth in West Yorkshire. The grim and forbidding moors which surrounded their parsonage home in the hillside village above the mill-filled valley of the Worth were perfectly suited to their tales of passionate and often unrequited love. No other authors are so closely associated with their home landscapes as the Brontë sisters – Charlotte, Emily and Anne – and no others, before or since, have captured the wild, wind-swept spirit of these bleak northern moors as well as they did in an extraordinary flowering of literary talent.

The three sisters, sometimes accompanied by their sickly and often drunken brother Branwell, often undertook long walks near their home, following the steep valley of the Sladen Beck across the cloughs and dikes to the brooding, wide-skied, tussock-grassed moorland above.

Another who sometimes went with them was Charlotte's friend Ellen Nussey, who later wrote:

> One long ramble made in these early days was far away over the moors to a spot familiar to Emily and Anne, which they called 'The Meeting of the Waters'. It was a small oasis of emerald green turf, broken here and there by small clear springs: a few large stones served as resting places; seated here, we were hidden from all the world, nothing appearing in view but miles and miles of heather, a glorious blue sky, and brightening sun. A fresh breeze wafted on us its exhilarating influence . . .

Emily's only novel, *Wuthering Heights*, published in 1847, is perhaps the most quintessential Brontë work, a towering masterpiece of human passion, perfectly matched to the wildness of its setting. In her preface to the 1850 edition, Charlotte explained the influence the moors had on her sister:

LEFT _____

*Looking north-west across the farmlands of Ape Dale from Ippikin's Rock on Wenlock Edge. The rock takes its name from the robber giant Ippikin, who is said to be entombed in a cave below the escarpment. He can apparently be recalled by reciting a doggerel·verse. The village in the valley is Hughley, the model for Housman's* A Shropshire Lad. *The poem refers to Hughley's steeple, but the church actually has a tower!*

To follow the footsteps of this extraordinary family, walk up the cobbled lane by their parsonage home and take the paved path marked 'Haworth Moor' which leads across the fields to West Lane. Fork left after about 45m (50yd) to the road which leads into the Penistone Hill Country Park. On the hillside to the left is Haworth Cemetery, while the hilltop village of Stanbury is prominent to the right above Lower Laithe Reservoir.

Crossing Moor Side Lane, take the path signposted 'Brontë Waterfalls' over a cattle-grid and onto a stone-walled lane which passes several deserted farmhouses and onto the open moor. Nearly all of these farms carry the name 'intake', showing that they were won, or 'taken in' from the moorland. The path, which can be boggy in places, now contours above the deep ravine cut by the Sladen Beck to descend to the Brontë Bridge, which was recently restored and replaced by means of an RAF helicopter. To the left up the narrow valley the famous Brontë Falls tumble down to join Sladen Beck. The Brontë Chair, a natural rock on the left of the path, is a good viewpoint for the falls. High up to the right, the windowless ruins of Virginia Farm overlook the scene.

Crossing the clapper slab of the Brontë Bridge, a path climbs steeply up through a gap in the wall where it is signposted 'Withins'. You now follow the right bank of South Dean Beck over Sandy Hill and past deserted circular sheepfolds, with the dark truncated shape of Top Withins guarded by its twin trees beckoning on the moor above. Crossing the beck, you climb up past two more abandoned farmhouses, also called Withins, until you reach the Pennine Way, which comes up from the right. The ruin of Top Withins, the probable model for Wuthering Heights, stands a few hundred yards to the left of the Way.

Follow the Pennine Way back down to its junction with South Dean Beck, then follow it east over Withins Slack and across Stanbury Moor beside Scar Hill. Over Flaight Hill and The Height, Ponden Reservoir appears in the valley of the River Worth to the left. Just before Upper Heights Farm, you leave the Way to descend via Far Slack Farm to reach Lower Slack and the reservoir. The grey stones of Ponden Hall, on the promontory to the left, is thought to be the model for Thrushcross Grange, home of Mr Lockwood and Nelly Dean in *Wuthering Heights*.

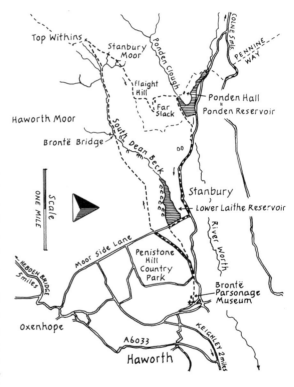

Turn right at the reservoir to the dam wall at its eastern end, where the path runs up to meet the Stanbury road at the eighteenth-century Ponden Mill. Follow the road which rises steeply to Stanbury. Pass through the ridge-top village and turn right on a minor road signposted 'Worth Valley Railway' and drop downhill to cross the Lower Laithe Reservoir dam wall. Bear left at the end of the wall and walk up the track above the water treatment works, which joins the Haworth road near the cemetery. Follow this back to the village.

ABOVE

*Approaching Top Withins, the isolated farmhouse thought to have been used as the location for* Wuthering Heights. *Wuthering is a northern word meaning cold and windy, and that is an apt description of the situation of Top Withins farmhouse. Sited on the edge of Delf Hill at about 1,300ft above the sea, it commands extensive views down South Dean Beck and across Stanbury and Haworth Moors*

PREVIOUS PAGE

*The ruined and deserted farmhouse of Upper Ponden stands remote and isolated above Ponden Clough on the path between Ponden Hall and Ponden Kirk on the bleak Haworth Moors. The gritstone crag of Ponden Kirk, high above the clough, is thought to have been the model for Penistone Crag in Emily Brontë's* Wuthering Heights. *Ponden Hall, now on the bank of the Ponden Reservoir, is the favoured location for Thrushcross Grange in the novel*

Ellis Bell (Emily) did not describe as one whose eye and taste alone found pleasure in the prospect; her native hills were far more to her than a spectacle; they were what she lived in, and by, as much as the wild birds, their tenants, or as the heather, their produce.

Charlotte wrote later: 'My sister Emily loved the moors . . . She found in the bleak solitude many and dear delights; and not the least and best-loved was – liberty.' That is a sentiment which Emily shared with generations of ramblers on these apparently inhospitable northern moors, and which can still be tasted by leaving the camera-clicking tourists on the 'Brontë Trail' behind in over-commercialised Haworth.

Properly equipped for the vagaries of moorland weather, you can follow in the footsteps of the Brontë sisters and visit that favourite Meeting of the Waters, now known as the Brontë Falls, and the ruined farmstead of Top Withins, reputedly the site of Heathcliff's home of Wuthering Heights. That pure-northern adjective is significant, as Emily explains in her introduction. It is, she says, descriptive of the atmospheric tumult to which its station is exposed in stormy weather. Pure, bracing ventilation they must have up there at all times, indeed: one may guess the power of the north wind, blowing over the edge, by the excessive slant of a few stunted firs at the end of the house; and by a range of gaunt thorns all stretching their limbs one way, as if craving alms of the sun.

Top Withins is reached by climbing to the trig point on Penistone Hill, the scene of Cathy and Heathcliff's childhood scramblings, and then descending above Lower Laithe Reservoir to the stone-slabbed 'Brontë Bridge' near the 'green oasis' of the Brontë Falls and following the South Dean Beck upstream. Today, it is a landmark registering the first 50 miles accomplished on Tom Stephenson's Pennine Way marathon. But it is also an inexplicably sad place, its roofless walls now insensitively capped with concrete, and its sightless windows staring blindly out over the scene which Emily may well have had in mind when she created Wuthering Heights. A plaque erected in 1964 by the Brontë Society 'in response to many inquiries' notes that the building, even when complete, bore no resemblance to the house she described.

Two lonely and gnarled sycamores only now bend when the north wind blows from Middle Moor Hill, Crow Hill and Great Wolf Stones, but the scene from Top Withins can still remind you of that seen by Cathy in *Wuthering Heights*:

On an afternoon in October, or the beginning of November, a fresh watery afternoon, when the turf and paths were rustling with moist, withered leaves, and the cold, blue sky was half-hidden by clouds, dark, grey streamers, rapidly mounting from the west and boding abundant rain . . .

## Daniel Defoe: Blackstone Edge

The Pennine moors, as already described, can create their own climate, as Daniel Defoe discovered on his *Tour Through the Whole Island of Great Britain* in 1725. Defoe, a cynical journalist probably best known for his novels *Robinson Crusoe*

and *Moll Flanders*, was also a keenly observant traveller. His tour of Britain during the reign of Queen Anne is widely regarded by historians as one of the most valuable insights into everyday life in the early eighteenth century. But for Defoe, as with many of those early travellers, the sight of hill country and 'natural' scenery was usually enough to throw them into a fit of the vapours. The Peak, for example, was to Defoe 'the most desolate, wild, and abandoned country in all England' and he was equally scathing about Westmorland, 'a country eminent only for being the wildest, most barren and frightful of any that I have passed over in England, or even Wales it self'. The moors were 'a waste and howling wilderness, over which when strangers travel, they are obliged to take guides, or it would be next to impossible not to lose their way'.

There was one occasion, however, when Defoe unwisely forwent the use of a guide, with almost disastrous consequences. He was travelling between Rochdale in Lancashire and Halifax in Yorkshire in August 1725, noting sarcastically 'for our great encouragement' as he set out that there was still snow on the mountains and that in some places the harvest had hardly been gathered in. Despite these omens, he embarked with three companions on what was to be an epic crossing of what he termed 'the Andes of England', via Blackstone Edge. Historically, the name Blackstone Edge was applied to most of the Lancashire moors. William Camden, in his *Britannia* published in the reign of Elizabeth I, described the Pennines as running 'through the middest of England'. From the south, the range was called 'Mooreland, after a while the Peak, Blackstone Edge, the Craven, the Stainmore and at length Cheviot'. Today, however, the name Blackstone Edge is usually applied to the smoke-blackened 472m (1,550ft) gritstone crest which frowns down over the mill chimneys of Littleborough and Rochdale.

There has been a crossing of the Pennines here via the aptly named Summit Pass at least since Roman times, and the 5m (18ft) wide paved causeway which mounts the moor below Blackstone Edge is still marked on modern maps as a Roman road. Photographs still regularly appear in guidebooks of this 'well-preserved Roman road', but the truth is, most of the well-graded paving stones that we see today probably only date from the 1734 Turnpike Act, which gave the authorities powers to 'widen the existing road over the craggy mountain of Blackstone Edge'.

The route is certainly older than that, however, and the first mention of it appears to be in the 1291 Patent Rolls of Edward I, when Hugh de Ellaund and Richard de Radclive were given grants for the repair across the 'causeway of Blacksteynegge'. There is, however, no evidence that the present surface is Roman, and indeed it corresponds very closely with other 'causeys' used by the packhorse 'jaggers' in the Pennines.

Twenty-six years before Defoe's classic encounter with Blackstone Edge, another intrepid traveller, Celia Fiennes, came this way by side-saddle, and appears to have used the 'Roman' road before its subsequent widening. 'Then I came to Blackstone Edge', she writes in her *Journeys Through England*. It was

> noted all over England for a dismal high precipice and steep in the ascent and descent on Either End; its a very moorish ground all about and Even just at the top, tho' so high, that you travel on a Causey wch is very troublesome as its a moist ground soe is usual on these high hills; they stagnate the aire and hold mist and raines almost perpetually.

Fiennes crossed the 'formidableness' of Blackstone Edge from the Yorkshire side into Lancashire, and was relieved to find the mists lessening as she descended the 'causey' towards Rochdale.

Travelling in the opposite direction twenty-six years later, Daniel Defoe found his fears beginning to rise with the wind as they mounted the snow-clad hills:

> It is not easy to express the consternation we were in when we came near the top of the mountain; the wind blew exceeding hard, and blew the snow so directly in our faces, and that so thick, that it was impossible to keep our eyes open to see our way. The ground also was so covered with snow, that we could see no track, or when we were in the way, or when out; except we were showed it by a fearful precipice on one hand, and uneven ground on the other; even our horses discovered their uneasiness at it; and a poor spaniel dog that was my fellow traveller, and usually diverted us with giving us a mark for our gun, turned tail to it and cried.

In the middle of this Blackstone 'white-out', Defoe was startled by a clap of thunder, the first he had ever heard in a snowstorm.

> Upon this we made a full stop, and coming altogether . . . we began to talk seriously of going back again to Rochdale, but just then one of our men called out to us, and said, he was upon the top of the hill, and could see over into Yorkshire, and that there was a plain way down on the other side.

After a few more adventures – Defoe reckoned he mounted to the clouds and descended to water level about eight times between Blackstone Edge and Halifax – they at last came into what he called a Christian country, a statement with which some Lancastrians might disagree.

Blackstone Edge holds few such terrors for the modern hill-walker. For Pennine Wayfarers striding north from the elegant M62 footbridge, this is easy walking, with stunning views across the glacial moraines of Clegg Moor and Red Scars Hill to the industrial landscapes of central Lancashire and the glittering waters of Hollingworth Lake, an eighteenth-century feeder reservoir for the Rochdale Canal which winds through the valley below. This is truly the top of the world hereabouts, and just south of the

RIGHT —————————————————————

*The so-called Roman Road which crosses Blackstone Edge from Littleborough near Rochdale, to Ripponden near Halifax on the other side of the Pennines, is now thought to be a packhorse causeway, restored as long ago as 1734. Early travellers such as Celia Fiennes and Daniel Defoe may have passed this way on their epic journeys through Britain in the seventeenth and eighteenth centuries. So too could the Romans, for the route is on a direct line between their forts at Littleborough in Lancashire and Aldborough, across the hill in Yorkshire*

# A ROUTE TO BLACKSTONE EDGE

Park at the White House Inn on the A58 Rochdale–Halifax road, which you cross, and walk down the Rochdale side for a few yards to join the Pennine Way (south) towards the prominent outcrop of Blackstone Edge. You pass through a series of disused quarries, including Blackstone Edge Delf, to climb out and over Blackstone Edge Moor, a barren expanse of peat hags and cotton grass. Climbing slowly through scattered boulders of gritstone on a sandy, silica-strewn path, you march on to a meeting of the tracks by the ancient Aiggin Stone, an old guide-post which now sadly has fallen.

Traverse right across the peat-hagged moor to reach the crags of Blackstone Edge, with its OS trig point 472m (1,550ft) perched incon-gruously on top of the rocks. The impressive rocky outcrop below is known as Robin Hood's Bed, although a more uncomfortable resting place would be difficult to find. Having admired the wonderful view from here, retrace your steps to the Aiggin Stone, and then turn left to wander down the old packhorse route. Just below the brow of the hill, which has a wonderful view down across Littleborough and the central industrial belt of Lancashire, you will come across the so-called Roman Road of Blackstone Edge. Whatever its age, it is a marvel of preservation, with its central grooved trough-stones, once thought to have been worn down by the brakes of Roman chariots. The views of the frowning escarpment of Blackstone Edge are very fine from here.

Retrace your steps up the causeway as far as the Broad Head Drain waterworks road, which contours across Blackstone Edge Pasture, following the concrete-lined regulating drain from Blackstone Edge Reservoir, across the A58. This leads easily back to the quarries near the White House where you began the walk.

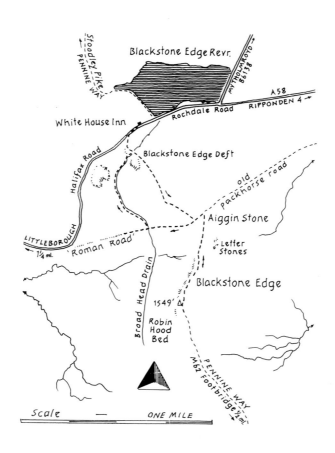

highest point, Robin Hood's Bed is a fine rocky bastion of gritstone, 'pot-holed and wrinkled like a elephant's skin', according to an old guidebook of mine.

At the crossing of the Pennine Way with the old 'Roman' packhorse route between Lancashire and Yorkshire stands the ancient guidepost known as the Aiggin Stone. Who or what 'Aiggin' was, no one knows, but there is an old legend concerning the stone-shifting Saxon god Aigle who is held responsible for a number of standing stones and tors in this part of the old kingdom of Brigantia.

The old way leads off east down Rag Sapling Clough where the stone paving finishes and is replaced by a natural rock surface, marked on old maps as Dhoul's Pavement, 'Dhoul' being the local dialect name for the Devil. The way passes beneath Fairy Hill on the right as it reaches the Rochdale road.

About 5 miles (8km) further north on the Pennine Way, a fine high level escarpment leads to the prominent monument which tops Stoodley Pike. This massively built 36m (120ft) gritstone obelisk was built in 1815 to commemorate the Peace of Ghent and Napoleon's abdication after the Battle of Waterloo.

So here, on this wind-swept edge of the Pennines, we encounter several of the recurring characters and themes of this book: the works of ancient man; Robin Hood; a mythical giant; Old Nick; and the eccentric whim of landowners to erect monuments on prominent viewpoints. All these have been our constant companions as we have searched out the high places to roam with a view.

---

| | FACTBOX | |
|---|---|---|
| | GR | MAP |
| Cat Bells, Cumbria | NY244198 | OL4 Lake District – N.W. Sheet |
| Yr Wyddfa, Gwynedd | SH610544 | OL17 Snowdonia – Snowdon |
| Eildon Hill North, Borders | NT555328 | LR73 Peebles & Galashiels |
| The Chains, Exmoor | SS735418 | LR180 Barnstaple & Ilfracombe |
| Maiden Castle, Dorset | SY670885 | LR194 Dorchester & Weymouth |
| Wenlock Edge, Shropshire | SO574968 | LR137 Ludlow & Wenlock Edge |
| Top Withins, Haworth, West Yorkshire | SD981354 | OL21 South Pennines |
| Blackstone Edge, West Yorkshire | SD974164 | LR109 Manchester |

# INDEX

Afanc of Glaslyn, 64, 162
Aiggin Stone, 186, 187
Ainsworth, Harrison, 85
Alfred, King, 130, 131
Alcock, Prof. Leslie, 72
Anglesey, 21; Monument, 127
Ape Dale (Wenlock Edge), 175,
    179
Arran, Isle of, 20
Arthur, King, 17, 52–3, 65, 68,
    70–3 *passim*, 78, 122, 162, 167;
    Seat, 53, 76–7, 78–9, *79*
Avalon, 72
Avebury, 132

Badbury Rings, 52
Badgworthy Hill/Water, 170, 172
Bagbury, 89
Bamburgh Castle, 35
Bannau Brycheiniog, 64, 65, *70*;
    Sir Gaer, 64, 65, *65*, *70*
Barley, 85; Moor, 85
Basalt, 35–7
Bat's Head, *49*, 51
Battle Abbey, 131
Beacon Hill (Charnwood Forest),
    21–4, *22*; (Warks), *133*, 135
Beinn Mhor (S. Uist), 16, *18–19*
Belas Knap, 136
Belknap, Edward, 134
Ben Macdhui, 52; – More, 16, *17*
Bennachie, Mither Tip, 96–102,
    *98–100*
Bennion, Charles, 21, 23
Berwyn Hills, 57; Moors, 164
Betws-y-Coed, 64
Birdlip, 136
Birds, 45, *45*, 48, 155
Black Mountains, *12–13*, 116, 164
Blackford Hill, Edinburgh, 78
Blackmore, R.D., 170
Blackmore Vale, 93, *93–5*, 174,
    *174*
Blackstone Edge, 32, *34*, 183–7,
    *185*
Blandford Forest, *97*

Bleaklow, 32
Bodbury Hill/Ring, *87*
Bonnie Prince Charlie, 125
Borrow, George, 162–5
Bosworth Field, 131
Bourne, Hugh, 153
Bradgate House/Park, 21, 23–4
Braid Hills, 78
Bratton Castle, 130; Down, 130,
    131
Brecon Beacons, *39–9*, 40–2, 116
Bredon Hill, 114, 116, *138–9*
Brendon Common, 173
Brightling Needle, 127
Brimham Rocks (Nidderdale), 24–
    7, *26–7*
British Camp (Malvern Hills),
    112–16, *113*, *115*
Broadway, 121, 135–7, *137–9*
Brontës, 179–83; Bridge, 180,
    183; Chair, 180; Falls, 180,
    182, 183
Bryant, Sir Arthur, 141
Bryn Myrddin, 65
Bulford Kiwi, 119
Burfa Camp, 89
Burke, Edmund, 156
Burnt Yates, 25
Bury Ditches, 89
Butterflies, 51, 90
Bwlch Glas, 68; – Main, 68;
    – Moch, 68
Bwlch-y-Saethau, 65, 68, *69*, 70–
    1, *71*

Cadbury Castle (Somerset), 20,
    53, 72, *72*, *74–5*, 173
Cadr Idris, 61–4, *62*, *63*
Caer Caradoc, 56, 57, *87*, 89, 179
Calton Hill, Edinburgh, 78, *79*
Camden, William, 90, 183
Carding Mill Valley, *87*
Carnedd Arthur, 71
Castle Hill, Edinburgh, 78
Castleton, 106, 110
Cat Bells, *158–9*, *160–1*, *161*

Cauldron Snout, 35
Cave Dale, 30
Caves, 30
Cerne Abbas Giant, 53, 119
Chains, The (Exmoor), 173
Chalk, 45–51, 119
Chase End Hill, 115
Chanctonbury Ring, 60, *88–9*
Charnwood Forest, 21–4
Cheddar Gorge, 30
Chesterton Windmill, Warwick,
    127
Child Okeford, 92
Cissbury Ring, 90–1, *91*
Citadel, Malvern Hills, 112, *113*
Civil War, 96, 131, 132, 135
Clapham, 111
Clappersgate, 9
Claxheugh Rock, 149
Clee Hills, 57, 135
Cleeve Common, 136
Clogwyn du'n Arddu, 68
Clowes, William, 153
Clubmen's Rising, 96
Clutter's/Giant's Cave, 114, 116
Cole, William, 117
Constable, John, 41, 117, 156
Coniston, Old Man of, 16, 54
Cook Monument, Easby Moor,
    143–7, *143*, *146*
Corn Du, 40, 41
Cornwall, 52, 53
Corston Hill, *72*
Corstorphine Hill, Edinburgh, 78
Cotswolds, 136, 137, *138–9*
Countryside Commission, 10,
    121, 124
Crag Lough, 35, 122, 124
Craig Cau, 61, *63*, 64
Craig-y-Dynas, 71
Craiglockhart Hill, Edinburgh, 78
Cranberry Rock (Stiperstones), *58*
Cratcliff Tor (Peak District), 80,
    81
Crib Goch (Snowdon), 66–7, 68,
    71

Cribyn, 40, 41
Croft Castle, 88; – Ambrey, 89
Cromwell, Oliver, 96, 135
Cross Fell (Pennine Way), 32, 35
Cuddy's Crag, 35, 122, 124
Cuillins, 35, 36
Cunliffe, Prof. Barry, 90, 96

Dancing Bear (Brimham), *25*, 26
Dassett Hills, 131, *133*, 134–5, *134*
Davies, Hunter, 124
Deerstones Quarry (Pendle), *84*
Defoe, Daniel, 11, 107, 183–7
Derwent Edge (Peak District), 110
Derwentwater, 160
Devil, 58, 60
Devil's Beef Tub, 60; Chair, 58, *59*; Chimney, 60, 136, *140*; Dingle, *55*; Dyke, 60; Nightcap, 60; Punchbowl, 60
Doone Valley, Exmoor, 170, *171*, 172
Dorset, 45–51, 91–6, 173–5
Druid's Idol (Brimham), 26; Writing Desk, 26–7, *27*
Dufton, 35
Durdle Door, *49*, 51, 173
Durham, Earl of, 147, 149
Durno, 97, *98–9*

East Anglia, 52, 116–17
Edale, 32, 106, 107; Skyline Walk, 106
Edge Hill, 131, 135
Edinburgh, 76–7, 78–9, *79*
Eggardon Hill, 174–5
Eildon Hills, 70, 165–70, *167–9*
Elgar, Edward, 112
Equipment, 17
Ethandun, 132, 133
Evesham, Vale of, 135, *138–9*
Exmoor, 170–3, *171*, *173*

Farleton Fell, 29–31, *30*
Fiennes, Celia, 11, 107, 184
Follies, 24, 127–55
Fovant Down, 119
Fox, George, 85
Friar's Crag (Lake District), *161*
Fuller, Mad Jack, 127

Gainsborough, Thomas, 117, 156
Gaping Gill (Ingleborough), 111, 112
Geoffrey of Monmouth, 53, 116

Geology, 21–51
Giant's Chair/Cradle/Pulpit, 53
Giants, 52–4 *passim*, 62 *see also individual headings*
Gilpin, William, 156
Glastonbury, 54, 73, 78, 173; Tor, 54, 72–3, *73*, 78, *191*
Glaslyn, 64, *66–7*, 70
Glenfinnan Monument, 125–7, *126*, *128–9*
Gog, Prince, 116
Gogmagog Hills, 52, 116–17, 119
Gordale Scar, *28*, 29, 30
Grasmere, 156, 157
Greenwich Park, 141–3, *141*, *142*
Grey, Lady Jane, 24
Grey Wife Syke (Ingleborough), 112
Grimes Graves (Brecklands), 90

Hadrian's Wall, 32, 35, *120*, 121–5, *123*
Hambledon Hill, 91–6, *93–5*, 173–4
Hardy, Thomas, 173–5
Hardy Monument, Blackdown Hill, 127
Harthill Moor (Peak District), 81
Hathersage, 81
Haworth Moors, 180, *181*, 182–3, *182*
Heaven Gate (Wrekin), 56, 57
Hell Gate (Wrekin), 56, 57; Gutter, 58
Herefordshire Beacon, 112, *113*, 116
Hermit's Cave (Peak District), 81
High Cup Nick, 31–5, *31*, *34*; Plain, 31
High Force, 35
Hillforts, 11, 20, 24, 52, 56, 57, 72, *74–5*, 78, 80, 87–118, *87*, *88*, 119, 130, 132, 136, 166, 167, 175 *see also individual headings*
Hindhead, 60
Hobbes, Thomas, 105
Hoccombe Combe, Exmoor, 170, *171*, 172
Hod Hill, 89, 92, 96, *97*
Hollybush Hill (Malverns), 115
Holyrood House, 76–7, 78
Hope Valley, 110
Horses, red, of Tysoe, *133*, 134; white, Alton Barnes, 132, Pewsey, 132, Uffington, 52,

119, Westbury, 130–2; *130*
Hotbank Crags, 124
Housesteads, 32, *126*, 122, *123*, 124
Housman, A. E., 54, 175–9
Howgill Fells, 31
Hull, Richard, 10, 127, Tower, 127
Hutton, William, 121, 124
Hutton Roof, 31

Idris Gawr, 53, 62; – ap Gwyddno, 62
Ingleborough, 31, *109*, 110–12, *110*
Ingleton, 21
Inkpen Beacon, 174
Ippikin's Rock (Wenlock Edge), *178*, 179

Jackman, Brian, 45
Jacobite rebellion, 125

'Karst', 30
Kilnsey Crag, 29
Kinder Scout, 32, 106
King's Play Hill, 131
Kipling, Rudyard, 122
Kirk Yetholm, 32

Lake District, 9–11, *14–15*, 31, 156–61
Lambton Worm, 149
Langdale Pikes, 9, 31
Langland, William, 11, 112
Layer, John, 117
Leith Hill, 10, 16, 127
Lethbridge, T. C., 116–17
Liddington Castle, 52
Limestone, 28–35
Limestone Corner (Hadrian's Wall), 124
Lindisfarne, 35
Llanaelhaearn, 103
Llanberis Pass, 68, 163
Llanrhaiadr, 164
Lliwedd, 70, 71, *71*
Llyn-y-Fan-Fach, 64–5, *65*, 70
Llyn Ffynnon Las, 64
Llyn-y-Gadair, 62, *62*, *63*
Llyn Llydaw, *11*, 64, *66–7*, 68–71, *71*
Long Mynd, 21, 56–8 *passim*, 61, *87*, 175, 179
Lose Hill (Peak District), 106, 107, 110

Loughrigg Fell, 9; Terrace, 157
Ludlow, 87
Lulworth Cove, 51, 173
Lune Gorge, 31

MacDonald, Alexander, 125
Maiden Castle, 89, 174
Malham Cove, 29, 30, 32
Malmsmead, Exmoor, 172, *173*
Malory, Sir Thomas, 52, 79
Malvern Hills, 21, 53, 57, 112–16, *113*, *115*, 135, *138–9*
Mam Tor (Peak District), 104–8, *107*, *108*, 110
Mawddach Estuary, 53, *62*, 64
McCaig, John Stuart, 153; Folly (Oban), 121, *150–2*, 153
Melbury Beacon, 92
Mercer, Roger, 91
Merlin, 65, 70
Merrick, The, *16*, 16
Middletongue Crag, *34*
Midsummer Hill (Malverns), 114, 116
Millstone grit, 24–7
Miner's Track (Snowdon), 66–7, 68, 69
Modred, 68, 70, 72
Moel Siabod, *11*, 64, 66–7, *71*
Monkhouse, Patrick, 104–5, 110
Monuments, 119–55, 187
Mothersole, Jessie, 122, 124
Mow Cop, 121, 153–5, *154*
Mycock, Solomon, 127

Nant Gwrtheyrn, 103; – Gwynant, 64, 68, 71
Naseby, 131
Navigation, 17, 20
Needle's Eye (Wrekin), 54, 56, 57
Newbiggin Crags, 31
Nichol Chair, *31*, 34, *34*
Nine Nicks of Thirlwall, 125; – Stones Circle (Peak District), 80, 81
Northrigg Hill (Hadrian's Wall), 125
Noyce, William, 112, 114
Nussey, Ellen, 179
Nutter, Alice, 85

Offa's Dyke, 42, 87
Old John's Tower, 23, 24
Old Man o'Mow, 153–4, *155*
Osmington, 45
Oxen Crag, Bennachie, *100*

Peak District, 30, 80–1, 104–8, 110, 145, 183–7 *see also individual headings*
Pen-y-Fan, *38–9*, 40, 41, *42*
Pen-y-Gadair, 61, *63*, 64
Pen-y-Gader-fawr, *12–13*, 16
Pen-y-ghent, 32, 54, 112
Pendle Hill, 81–5, *83*, *84*; Forest, *83*
Penistone Hill, 183
Penn Hill, 136
Pennine Way, 31–5, *33*, 85, 180, 183–7
Penshaw Hill/Monument, 147–9, *147*, *149*, 153
Pevsner, Sir Nikolaus, 137
Pewsey, 130, 132
Pinnacles, Inaccessible and Weasel (Peak District), 81, *82*
Ponden Kirk (Haworth), *182*
Portland, Isle of, 45, *46–7*, *50*
Portway (Peak District), 80, 81
Potter, Beatrix, 160
Poucher, Walter, 61
Pre-Cambrian, 21–4
Pumlumon, 42; Fawr, 64, 164
Pyg Track, Snowdon, 66–7, 68

Queen Camel, 72
Queen's House, Greenwich, 142
Quiraing, The, 36, 37, 40; Needle, 37, 40; Prison, 37, 40; Table, 40

Radway Castle, 135
Raggedstone Hill (Malverns), 115
Raven Scar (Ingleborough), *109*
Red Earl's Dyke (Malverns), 112, 114–16 *passim*
Richard's Castle, 88
Ridgway, 52
Ringstead, 48, 173
Robin Hood, 17, 53–4, 80–1
Robin Hood's Bed, 186, 187; Cave, 81; Stride, 80–1, *82*
Rollright Stones (Cotswolds), 60
Romans, 57, 80, 81, 87, 89, 90, 96, 97, 101, 104, 112, 121–4, *123*, 167
Rooke, Major, 26
Roseberry Topping (Easby Moor), *143*, 146
Roundway Down/Hill, 131, *132*
Rowtor Rocks (Peak District), 81
Royal Naval College, 142

Royal Observatory, 142
Ruskin, John, 156

Safety, 17
Salisbury Crags, Edinburgh, 76–7
Saltway, 114
Sanctuary, The (Skye), 36–7, 40
Sandstone, 37–45
Scafell, 9, *14–15*, 16
Scotland, 16, 17, *17–19*, 21, *34*, 35–7, 78–9, 96–103, 125–9, 150–3, 165–70 *see also individual headings*
Scott, Sir Walter, 165
Sewingshields Crag (Hadrian's Wall), 53, 70, *120*, 122, 124
Shaftesbury, 92, 96, 174, *174*
Shropshire, 21, 54–61, 175–9 *see also individual headings*
Siller Stane (Eildons), 166
Skye, 35–7, *37*, *36*, 40
Smailholm Tower, 165
Snowdon, *11*, 16, 64, 65, 68–71, *71*, *104*, 162–5, *162*, *163*
Solomon's Temple, Grin Low, 127
Somerset, 20, 53, 54, 60, 72, 73, 78, 170–3; Levels, 54, *72*, 78; *see also individual headings*
St Joseph, Prof. J. K., 96–7
St Michael's Mount, 52, 53
Stanage Edge (Peak District), 81
Standton Drew, 60
Stanton Moor, 81
Stephenson, Tom, 31, 32, 85, 183
Stevenson, Robert Louis, 78
Steyning Gap, 91
Stiperstones, 58–61, *58*, *59*
Stokesay Castle, 88
Stoodley Pike (Pennines), 32, 187
Storr, The, 35–7, 52; Old Man of, *35*, 36–7, *36*, 52
Sugar Loaf, Dallington, 127
Swinyard Hill (Malverns), 114
Swithland Wood (Charnwood), 24
Swyre Head (Dorset), 51
Symond's Yat, 42–5, *43*, *44*

Tal-y-llyn, 61, 64
Tan Hill (Pennines), 32
Tarn Hows, 160
Thomson, James, 121
Timperley, H. W., 54
Todd Crag (Lake District), 9

Top Withins (Haworth), 180, *181*, 182, 183

Towers, *10*, 121, 127, 135, 150–5 *see also* Follies; Monuments

Traprain Law, *101*, *102*, 102–3

Trecobben Hill (Cornwall), 53

Tre'r Ceiri, 103–4, *104*, *105*

Trotternish, Skye, 35–7 *passim*

Trow Gill (Ingleborough), 111

Turner, J. M. W., 156

Tyle Gwyn, 65

Tyndale Monument, 136

Uffington, 52, 119

'Vale of the Little Dairies', 92, 96, 174

Wade, Charles, 137

Wade's Causeway, 53

Waghorn, Tom, 16

Wainwright, Alfred, 9, 160

Wales, *11–13*, 21, *38–9*, 40–2, 61–71, 103–5, 162–5 *see also individual headings*

Wallace Monument, Abbey Craig, 127

Wandlebury, 20, 53, 116–17

Ward, G. H. B., 106

Ward, James, 156

Washington Wild Fowl Trust, 148

Watkin, Sir Edward, 68; Path, 68, 71

Webb, Mary, 60, 61

Wenlock Edge, 56, 57, 87, 175, *176–8*, 178

Wessex, 173–5

Weymouth, 48

Whillans, Don, 37

Whin Sill, 31–5, 121, 122, 124

Whipp, Arnold, 16

Whipsnade Lion, 119

White Nothe, *46–7*, 48, *50*; Peak, 81, 110; Rocking Stone, 26

Whitehorse Hill (Oxon), 16

Wilbraham, Randle, 153

Wild Edric, 61

Wilderhope, 88, 175

Williamson, Henry, 170

Wills Neck (Quantocks), 174

Wilmington, Long Man of, 119

Win Hill (Peak District), 20, 110

Windermere, Lake, 9

Winnats Pass (Peak District), 30, 110

Winshields, 124, 125

de Wint, Peter, 156

Wistman's Wood (Dartmoor), 145

Witchcraft, 85

Wolfe Monument, *142*, 143

Woodhouse Eaves (Charnwood), 23

Worcestershire Beacon, 114, 116

Wordsworth, William, 10, 156–7

Wrekin, The, 54–7, *55*, *57*, 175, 179

Wyns Tor (Peak District), 81

Yorkshire Dales, 21, 24–31, 109–12; Moors, 143–7, *143–6 see also individual headings*

Youlgreave, 81

Yr Eifl, 103, *104*; – Wyddfa, *11*, 64, 69, 70, 71, 162, *162*, 163

Ystrad-gwyn, 61, 64

Zig-Zags, Snowdon, 68

*Midsummer's Eve at Glastonbury Tor*

191

ACKNOWLEDGEMENTS
Many people have helped me, advertently
or inadvertently, in the preparation of
this book, but I would like to thank
particularly John Cleare and Mark
Richards for their inspiration and
companionship; my colleague Ken Smith,
chairman of the Hill Fort Study Group,
for his considerable help and advice on
Chapter 3; Wendy Fellingham of the
Ordnance Survey for cartographic
confirmations; Tom Waghorn for his
long-distance view charts, and John
Beckwith, who was there at the
beginning.